"Up West" on Prince Edward Island

Life in the Early Nineteen-hundreds

Everett Platts

Copyright ©2016 by J. Wallace Platts

"Up West" on Prince Edward Island
Life in the Early Nineteen-Hundreds

All Rights Reserved. No part of this book may be reproduced, stored in a retrieval system, or transmitted in any form or by any means—electronic, mechanical, photocopy, recording, or otherwise—without the prior permission of the publisher or author. The only exception is by a reviewer, who may quote short excerpts in a review.

Natural copyright 1988

ISBN: 978-0-9971694-9-2

Contact CLM Publishing
E: clmpublisher@gmail.com

Published by CLM Publishing

Printed in the United States of America

INTRODUCTION

(... by the typist of the 1988 limited edition (six copies)
"Stories of My Life")

Father is a storyteller. His stories are true. These are some of the stories he told us boys as we were growing up on Prince Edward Island in the 1940s and '50s.

In 1977, when Father had his seventy-second birthday, I gave him a "Nothing Book," a blank bound book that was popular in the bookstores at the time. Eventually he filled it with these marvelous stories of his youth and adventures.

Father is a letter writer, too, and as I type the stories from the handwritten book it's as if I'm reading one of the weekly letters from home (except the penmanship is a little neater, thank goodness). But the stories fly through the pages in that same effortless way the rest of us slave to achieve.

The first time I picked up the partly finished book was during a vacation visit home. I read a chapter and then called my daughter, Katie, who might have been 16 at the time. I offered to read a chapter or two out loud and we settled down on the chesterfield. Ninety pages later, there were no more pages to read so we had to stop. We were entranced. I hope others will be, too.

Father was born in 1905 near Kildare Cape, Prince Edward Island. He married my mother, Belle MacNeill, in 1929.

Wallace Platts
Calgary, Alberta, Canada
December 1988

INTRODUCTION

(…to this formal publication, 2016, by W. Platts)

Only six copies (typed, photocopied) were bound by a bookbinder in Calgary, Alberta, in 1988, and given to Father and Mother and the immediate family. Father was very pleased with the result but was also a bit shy about it, thinking the stories were only of family interest. He didn't realize they went some way to capturing a place, an age, and the marvel of growing up on a farm in western Prince Edward Island in the early part of the twentieth century.

My parents both died in their early 90s in a Charlottetown nursing home in 1998. These stories live on, and deserve to be made available to a wider audience. They are stories of horses, pets, foxes, inventions, cars, machines, boats, and family life in Prince County, Prince Edward Island, and later, on the outskirts of Charlottetown, PEI, which the family reached by horse and wagon, as you will read in these pages.

Cayman Brac,
Cayman Islands
2016

PREFACE

The reader can blame Wallace and Edna for this book. It is being written on their suggestion. Wallace suggested quite a number of chapter titles.

However, he wasn't able to suggest at what point in my life I would commence. That will be my decision.

I also had some misgivings about starting at all. I have not been one to remember or take account of dates or years. Unless I find old records, or have family help, some incidents may not be identified by the year in which they took place.

I will go back in time to some early recollections, and as near as possible will keep things in chronological sequence.

For what it is worth, I dedicate this book to my wife and children.

Everett Platts
'Tween Tides
New Dominion
Prince Edward Island
1978 (handwritten)

Chapter 1

I was born in St. Felix, a community about three miles south of Tignish, where my father was born and where he farmed.

My earliest recollection was of climbing a woodpile, with Father's help, to catch a fleeting view of the train as it pulled out of Tignish and through Harpers. We could often hear its whistle and see the black smoke from the steam locomotive.

Apparently there were no upstairs windows that faced in the right direction in our house, but from the top of the woodpile I did get a view of this train, which I can clearly remember.

Before this time, and probably before I could walk, I got the little finger of my right hand caught in the cog gear of the hand-wringer that mother was turning. Mother grabbed me up and ran to a kindly neighbor, Mrs. Roc, who my parents told me when I was older, took care of both of us.

Mother was young and had had rheumatic fever after I was born. Dad had been born and brought up in this wholly French district. Mother, on the other hand, had been born in Greenmount and was not bilingual.

I never knew this kindly woman by anything but Mrs. Roc. The 1880 atlas shows this property as belonging to Roche Chaisson. Apparently Mother went to her with many problems.

The scar on my finger still remains.

In my early life our family moved to Kildare Cape, where Dad bought a large farm. He also retained a sixty-acre farm in St. Felix, or Little Tignish. There were no buildings on this farm.

About this time I was taken by Aunt Carrie Treat to Hartford, Connecticut. I was near six years old and went to kindergarten for a few months.

While going to and from this school, I had an experience that taught me to admire and respect all policemen.

When coming home from school one day, I ran across an intersection cornerwise. A policeman blew a fierce blast on his whistle. I didn't realize it was meant for me until some other children told me. I was sure rattling in my shoes as I went back to this large cop. However, he was so very kind. He stood behind me with his hands on my shoulders and asked me a lot of questions. When he found out I was from Prince Edward Island he was especially nice. He gave me careful instructions on the proper way to cross street corners, and a friendly pat, and let me go. I often saw him on the same corner and we exchanged friendly waves. Although his advice was probably the same as was given me by my Aunt Carrie, his was what I always recalled.

Dad, as previously mentioned, had been born and brought up in a French district. He and his two sisters were fluently bilingual. Mother knew but little French and we only heard Dad speak in this language when he was talking to our French neighbors. He knew some French songs, one of which he often sang while working around the farm.

He continued to sing this song frequently through the years. However, as we grew up, and the girls especially started to study French in school, he stopped singing his song. Sometimes he would start off with the first few words, then check himself. And we never got him to sing it after.

Dad often told of an experience he'd had at or before the time of my birth. They had contacted a family in Miminegash and had hired a daughter to come as a housekeeper. Dad went after her on a certain day, with a horse and wagon, of course. The daughter and suitcases were in and ready to go. All their conversation had been in English. The girl's mother said good-bye to her in English, then in French she said, "Don't let those damned Protestants work you too hard."

"Don't worry," said Herbert, also in French. "We will take good care of her." They all three had a good laugh, and Mother said the girl was a fine one, and that she and her family were friends for years.

Due to lack of use, Dad eventually lost his ability to converse in the second language.

Grandfather Platts lived with us at "The Capes" for a number of years. However, I have very few memories of him.

One memory, though, is in regard to a repeating cap pistol given me one Christmas by a storekeeper in Tignish, Mr. Shelfoon by name. I was too young and not strong enough to fire it. Pulling the trigger worked some mechanism in the thing that forced the hammer back and pushed up a fresh cap from a roll. As you continued to pull the trigger, the hammer came down and *Bang!* I had to get my grandfather to fire it for me. He would hold his arm off to one side, turn his head the other way and close his eyes. Then *Bang!*

My grandfather went to live with Aunt Carrie in Hartford, and was there when he died. He and Grandmother Platts, together with a sister and several brothers, are buried at the Church of England cemetery at Kildare Cape.

Great Uncle Thomas Platts, d. Nov. 23, 1883
Church of England, Kildare Cape

Chapter 2

KILDARE CAPE

Our farm at Kildare Cape was quite large, quite level, and partly wooded. A brook ran across the farm near each end, and a couple of good wells or pumps gave adequate provision for watering livestock.

Some of the fences were built on low dikes, especially the line fences. On top of this dike, the early settlers had laid a large cedar log; then crossed stakes supported a second, smaller log.

Since these fences were very old, the large logs were often hollow from end to end, and a fine place for birds' nests, toads, squirrels, and snakes. We eventually replaced these fences with posts and wire. The cedar logs made fine kindling.

On a recent visit to this farm, now largely overgrown with spruce trees, I located parts of these dikes. The farm buildings and house were destroyed by fire. However, a German couple have built a fine house in a heavily wooded area where we had raised many, but poor, crops. The fields were sandy and would only produce well if fertilized. And the fields close to the barns got the best of the only fertilizer available in those days.

MUSSEL MUD

This is what we called the mud dug up from the bottom of bays and rivers; it contained large amounts of oyster shell. We hauled as much as we could from Cascumpec Bay, a haul of about 12 miles by ice in the winter but much farther in the summer.

The value of this mud can be appreciated somewhat when one considers the toil and long hours we put in to get it. Just to see the crops it would help to produce, and over so long a time, was all a farmer needed to justify the work involved.

Dad would be up very early and have the horses fed. We would have an early breakfast, do up some of the necessary chores, hitch up two teams and be off. The "board ice" was a strip of ice inside the heavy ice that would ground on sand bars offshore a few hundred yards. We would follow the road down to where Jacques Cartier Park is now located, then take the ice to Alberton and on to Cascumpec.

Dad's reason for the early start was to get in first at the digger. Then we would haul the first loads to shore and bank it, to be hauled home by wagons in the summer. By the time we would get the two loads shoveled off we would fall in behind a long line at the digger and wait our turn for our second load each.

Then off for home. This mud was very heavy and could only be hauled this distance when the roads were good. One day we got caught in a severe snowstorm. (There were no weather forecasts back then.) The horses were so tired when we got home that old Parker (more later) laid down in the snow when we stopped in the field where we unloaded the mud in small piles to be spread in the spring.

This old horse was one of my team. I asked Dad what I should do. He told me to unload as usual. When I had a pile unloaded, I picked up the reins and spoke to the horses. Parker immediately got to his feet and went ahead until I stopped them. Then he again laid down.

The next time up he stayed up. He seemed none the worse when we got them in the stable. But they all four sure got a good rubdown and a good dinner.

I have never heard of a horse doing this. He sure must have been leg-weary.

Parker was a fine old animal. As wise as a crow. We used him for all our one-horse jobs. Or most of them. He knew "Gee" and "Haw" as well as "Gettap" and "Whoa." When using him in a scuffler to weed or hill potatoes I would often leave the reins home. He was so used to the work that he would go right breast-up to the fence at the end of a row, turn right or left as I directed by word, and down the next row.

Either at noon or in the evening I would get on his back to go home. If the stable door was open, no amount of whoa-ing would stop him, so I would put my hands against the top of the door frame and slide off over his rump.

One fine spring day, Mother wanted to go to her sister's on the next farm. We generally walked the short distance through the woods. However, everything was in flood, so Dad hitched Parker in a box sleigh for Mother this time. She took off out the lane but in a few minutes, back she came. There was a hollow between our farms and there was quite a freshet of water running across the road. Parker refused to cross it; he just turned around and came home.

Dad jumped in the sleigh, picked up the reins, and when they came to the water, the old horse never hesitated! He sure knew who was in the driver's seat.

A QUEER PET

Parker was always used as the "furrow" horse. One very cold morning as I was making the first round in plowing a large field that went from the pond to the shore, the horses suddenly stopped opposite the gate that came in through the long side of the field. I thought they wanted to go home. I spoke to them and they started, but only went a few steps before they stopped again. This time I noticed that Parker was the first to stop. I thought his collar might be uncomfortable so I went forward to examine it.

When I got to his head I saw a muskrat running ahead in the furrow. I knew what was wrong. Parker wouldn't step on the little animal.

I was wearing a sheepskin-lined leather coat. I took it off and threw it over the beautiful animal. I then picked him up by the tail and carried him as I continued to plow.

When we got in the shelter of the woods that bordered the pond, I turned the horses so that their backs were to the wind. Then I ran with my treasure the quarter-mile home. We had a large milk can used to send milk to a factory at one time, but now it was worn-out and leaky. I put the muskrat into this and back I ran to the field, urged to hurry by Dad, who didn't know the precautions I had taken with the team. They had not moved.

At noon I transferred the fellow to a more comfortable enclosure and gave him water and a carrot. He very shortly became quite tame and before long could be handled like a cat or dog.

A friend of ours, Perley Haywood, had muskrats in his basement, where he hoped to raise them ranch-style. So I eventually gave him mine, hoping to get a pair of young ones. Perley's basement was clay, and the rats had dug in at one place. He thought they had a den in the hole. His house was a few hundred yards from his mill pond and the muskrats eventually dug their way free.

For a long time they would return and eat all the food given them. After the first spring, he didn't see them again.

ANOTHER PET

My first suit with long pants had a vest I wore at work. One day as I went through one of the large shore fields I saw a crow that didn't seem to fly when it should have. I went closer, and it only ran.

I caught it and carried it home, held snugly against my body. I took the crow into the kitchen and put it on the floor. The crow ran under the couch.

Then Mother yelled at me to get out of the house. "Look at yourself!" she said. My dark-blue vest was shiny with lice! I took my outer clothes off and hung them on the fence.

In the house, Mother was feeding the crow with bread crumbs in front of the lounge. As soon as she backed away a bit he would come out and eat.

We had some de-lousing powder for our hens, which I used on the crow. I put him in a suitable pen. As soon as he got rid of the lice and was well fed he was able to fly as well as any crow. He became very tame and when I released him he refused to leave. Needless to say, I didn't try to drive him off.

I could always call him to my hand for food, or he would come to my head or shoulder as I walked outside.

However, he must have been quite old, as he died during the first winter.

RED SQUIRRELS

One spring I saw a squirrel coming out of a hole in a large spruce tree. I had thought this hole was a flicker's nest. (We used to call them yellowhammers.) With a pair of heavy leather gloves I caught three young squirrels, almost full-grown.

I sold one to Irene Wells and kept two for myself. I gave them the run of my bedroom. I fed them, and they had a nest in a large box.

They became very tame, and I could go anywhere with them in my coat pocket.

I took one to Tignish with me one day. The clerks in Myrick's store could coax it out onto the counter for a nut. It would grab it, then run quickly back into my pocket. It would leave the nut there and pop its head out to look for more.

Each time the clerk would get further away down the counter with the food, and the squirrel would timidly venture by little short runs and stops, grab the nut, and come back to me with one long swift run. Eventually she coaxed the pet the full length of the counter.

In the meantime, I had backed away quite a distance from the other end of the countertop. So when the squirrel came racing back with the nut and made a jump for me he just barely made the bottom of my pant leg, and quickly climbed it and found himself under my coattail. Everyone had a great laugh as he would peek through the coat bottom trying to find his way to my pocket.

We often saw squirrels running over the roof of our house but thought they were other wild ones. One day I was able to coax one of these to me, and it immediately ducked into my pocket. The investigation uncovered a hole in the window screen hidden from my view by a partially drawn blind. It being summer, the window was propped open a few inches. The little fellows had been coming and going for goodness knows how long.

For a while they would always be in their box at night but by the end of summer they had become wild.

Irene had lost her squirrel. Their dog had killed it. When she went to clean out his box she found quite a hoard of nuts hidden in a corner. She buried her pet in what she designated a pet graveyard and erected a fancy marker.

FIELD MICE

During harvest, I often caught field mice. I caught a very heavy one and found it quite tame. In fact, it wouldn't jump off my outstretched hand until I lowered it almost to the ground. She was very pregnant.

Again the zinc-lined tea box was put into good use, this time with lots of straw and chaff, etc. I would rush home from school (one mile) at noon to look for a litter and again at three thirty.

One noon there was a bunch of little pink mice. However, in the evening I found that they were dead. I guess too much handling had scared the mother so that she didn't nurse them. She had made a nest and was eating well.

One time we were hauling in turnips. Florence and Emily (my sisters) were helping and were in the cart, with Dad driving. I came in head-first over the tail of the cart and a mouse I had in my pocket dropped out. It's a wonder the girls didn't jump out over the wheel. They sure made as much fuss as if it had been a snake. The poor little mouse never heard such shrieks and must have been glad to get back in the darkness of my pocket.

Girls sure are funny.

Another time, Father and Mother being away for the afternoon, Florence and I were "hosting" a small party, the occasion being my birthday. As we were all singing around the piano with Florence playing, I slipped a small toad down her back.

She near went into hysterics as the toad went down wiggling near to her waist. She ran out on the veranda and with the help of some girls, stood on her head against a post until the offending thing fell out. I guess the party was kind of spoiled, for Florence at least.

Speaking of such small animals and reptiles, I remember when Dad decided to divide one of the large twenty-acre shore fields into two.

We dug a row of post holes down one side of the field to the halfway point to make a lane, then across the field to the line fence. For some reason we didn't get the posts in for some time, and almost daily I took it upon myself to go down and run along this row of holes, examining each for toads, frogs, mice, or snakes that might have fallen in.

I had a queer love for those creatures and released them all; and was glad when we eventually got the posts in and the holes filled up.

As I view mouse damage now to pine trees I set out 10 years ago, I sure have changed in my regard for field mice.

MY FIRST GUN

I had been bugging my parents for some time to let me buy a .22 rifle.

One winter morning after a very heavy snowfall, I brought the subject up again while Dad and I took turns pumping water for the horses.

Mother had thrown scraps out the back door and a hen had left the barnyard and flown about halfway to the house, then had fairly well bogged down in the soft, new snow.

Father put the proposition to me. "Each of us make a snowball," he said. And if I came closer to the hen than he, I could buy the rifle. I threw first and came fairly close. Dad threw and hit the poor hen squarely. Then he went on pumping.

Subject closed.

SHEEP

We always had quite a flock of sheep, so we had to keep all fences in good repair. Once in a while they would get through or under a fence, or through a gate left open for the cattle to go or come from the large sheltered spring below the road.

For a few years we had a ram that was fairly cross. Mother and Florence were the only ones really afraid of him.

We often got Emily to go for the sheep if they got away very far. She would tease the ram, then quickly dodge aside as he came at her, grab his wool, and get on his back. She could then direct him home and the sheep would follow.

I had a pair of stilts, and would often tease the ram when he was some distance from me. He would make a few leaps of rage, then come racing at me. When he lowered his fine head to finish me off, all he would see was the stilt legs and he would skid to a halt.

One spring, Father bought a young ram, well bred, to introduce new blood into the flock. The old fellow was put in the large outside fox ranch.

The sheep were at the back of the farm but came home through the night. The lane ran along one side of the fox ranch. The old fellow butted his way out through the heavy-gauge fox wire.

The two rams were squaring off for what would probably have been a fight to the finish when we found them. And there was no doubt about which would have been the victor. All we had to do was look at how the fox wire was stretched before it finally gave way.

HORSES IN GENERAL

We had from four to six horses. One mare had a foal each year, and one spring both this mare and a daughter of hers had foals from the same horse. They were as like as two peas. We had a new two-seated driving wagon and were looking forward to having a matched team.

Father bought a wonderful set of driving harness with a lot of patent leather, divided reins, colored spreaders, and lots of bright chrome or nickel-plated buckles.

When the young horses were two years old they were pastured in the shore field, which had a wooded area, and the fine spring and brook for water.

One day, Dad suggested that I run down and see if both colts were okay. He said that he hadn't seen both of them at one time for a couple of days.

When I came close to the woods, I saw both the animals fairly close together. One appeared to have been lying down and was just getting up. First I started to go home to report all was well, but then I noticed that the one that was getting up was in the same position. When I got closer, I found that this beautiful animal had been hung on an old rope swing left between two trees by children of a family that Dad had rented a plot of land to some years earlier.

Nothing in my young life bothered me any more than having to go home with this news to my father.

All he said after a few minutes with his back turned to me was, "Get a couple of knives while I hitch a horse in the drag sleigh, we might get the hide."

We didn't skin the colt. He had been too long dead.

To go back to the double-seated wagon.

Each summer after the crop was in, we would pick a fine Sunday and drive to Uncle Jim Platts' in Howlan. As there were five of us, we would use two driving wagons, one with a buggy, and one with a parasol that could be erected to give shade from the midday sun.

This was a terrific day for all concerned. Uncle Jim (Father's uncle) was a very fine farmer. When we arrived, the women would go to the house, but I would help Dad and Uncle Jim take care of the two horses.

Then all the stock and most of the farm would be gone over. The age of all new, and some not-so-new calves and both their parents' names would be told. Litters of pigs, sheep, foals, etc., would be looked at and described. Then around the fields we would walk. This field of grain was sown on such and such date, when the moon was in such and such a quarter, and sown for so many bushels to the acre, and so many pounds of clover, hay, or other seed. This was the hayfield that had yielded so many loads per acre last year, and so on and on.

But this certain trip was to be a very special one. We had this wonderful new wagon with the fine harness. Of course, we didn't have a matched team; that would come later. The team we did have were good, strong animals and rode along fairly well.

So off we went, in fairly fine style. However, as we turned out from our lane to the main road, the pole between the two horses broke off short. We had to take the fine new rig back to the barn, take off all the shiny new harness, dress the horses up in the old rigs, and go to Howlan the same old way.

The broken pole was judged by the dealer to be defective and it was eventually replaced. It was so long in coming, however, that a clever neighbor, Dan Getson, made one for us. We removed all the iron fittings from the broken pole and put them on the homemade one. All was then painted, striped, and varnished, and as far as I can remember the new pole was put away when it arrived and never used.

THE "FOX MEAT" HORSE

One spring, for some reason or other, we were short of a horse. Father was always on the lookout for old animals for fox meat. This spring he found a large, rangy, ugly, off-white horse at Norway, a community north of Tignish.

Such a thin animal I never had seen. And he didn't have a tooth in his head. Not much fox meat on his frame. So Dad started to put some meat on the bones.

He boiled oats and other food for him, and we soon found out that this was a super horse. He was a fast walker, strong and willing. As gentle and kind as a kitten, too, and he soon began to put on weight. We used him all through the summer and for the fall plowing, and really got fond of him.

We were all very sorry when autumn came and he had to go for the purpose intended.

I forgot when writing about Parker to mention how many times my sisters and I used this old horse to go visiting in the long winter months, knowing that he would bring us safely home.

We had a box sleigh, steep-sided, and we would have it loaded with clean straw and lots of buffalo robes.

I would sit up and drive through the winter roads to visit relatives or friends in Greenmount. When it was time to go home, we would start off at a good clip. But we would get sleepy and cold. Then I would put the reins over the dashboard and snuggle down in the rugs.

Immediately Parker would slow to a walk. But we knew and trusted him. When all noise and squeak of runners on the snow stopped, we knew we were home, or that there was a sleigh coming from the opposite direction. In this case Parker would find a suitable place and pull off the road and stop, sometimes half a mile before the other traveler met us.

Sometimes I would get up and take over, and probably speak to the other people. Other times I wouldn't. Often people spoke of meeting us on the road when we knew nothing about it.

Father and Mother would be watching for us and sometimes would come to help me unhitch and put the sleigh in the machine shed, and the horse in the stable.

WORK ON A FARM

Father had been born with the heel on one leg attached to the buttock. An operation to straighten this out was delayed until he was a few months old. This leg was always quite thin, and a bit shorter than the other one.

When he bought a pair of boots or shoes he would take a layer or two of one shoe and put it on the other one. Even so, he would tire quicker than other men when following a team all day.

He had a harrow cart for use behind spring-tooth and spike harrows, and would use an extra horse. He had also bought a beautiful "sulky plow." Neither he nor the servicemen from the Oliver company could ever get it to make both sods the same. So Dad condemned it to use in the back or shore fields where no one would see the botched job. The light Massey gang plow was used around the buildings and within sight of the lane or road.

When I was nine years old I was able to do the plowing and was kept out of school to do it. The riding plow was stored away in the back of the machine shed. Of course, Father would have to break out the ridges and finish them up, too. And he would fix fences, or he could do any work around the barn and keep an eye on me.

This plow had straight coulters and occasionally a stone would lodge between the point of the shear and the coulter. I wasn't strong enough to pull the plow back to kick the stone out. If the unplowed area was wide enough I could lever the plow out and turn the team out on the sod, get another stone and knock the offending one out, and bring the team back to working position again. However, if there wasn't room to do this without defacing the plowed area, I had to call for help. Thank goodness the next year I was able to pull the plow back alone.

Once in a while, Dad would come and make a couple of rounds to straighten out my furrow. He told Mother that if I went any further I would have the furrow so crooked that a snake would break its back trying to follow it.

Dad also plowed the headlands after the field proper had been finished. As I got older I became more independent and could work all day alone.

Working the "other" farm, as we called the sixty acres at Little Tignish, was a lonesome job. Mother would pack two lunches, dinner and supper, for me, and we'd put two meals for the horses in the truck wagon box and away we would go, the horses and I, until dark.

There was good water at the two ends of this farm but if I was working in the middle fields I would take a thirty-gallon milk can full of water. We had individual oat boxes for the horses, and lots of hay and a bag of oats made up my load.

At meal time I would tie a horse to each wheel, then water and feed them. I also unharnessed them completely to let their shoulders cool. Then I would get a comfortable place and eat my meal.

After my supper meal I would work until just before dark, then hitch two horses to the wagon, take the harness off the third and turn him loose. The horses were also keen to get home. The one turned loose would be home long before we arrived, to let the folks know we were coming.

THE TRACTOR

One day as I was spike harrowing in the large field next to the road at the "other" farm, there was a man operating a tractor in the adjacent field. I was using four horses and the harrow cart. I was very curious to get a look at the tractor. I had never seen one up close before. However, we worked nearly all day without coming close together at the line fence.

But as I came up to the fence along about four o'clock, the machine was heading exactly to that point. I turned the four horses and stopped to wait. I got off the cart and went over to the fence.

When the operator got close, he started to wave. I thought he sure was friendly until I noticed an urgency in his actions and that he was pointing at me. I turned to look behind me; the four horses had taken fright at the unfamiliar noise and were running away.

All the shouts of "Whoa!" were to no avail. The cart and harrows were bouncing all over the place and eventually broke clear. Tie ropes between the horses broke and they went off in different directions.

Luckily, the gate at the road was closed so they couldn't get home. I was able to salvage enough gear to hitch two horses only. The field was nearly done and without the cart, I finished it before too long.

I never did see the tractor, and Father had every reason to be a bit sarcastic. It was a miracle that none of the horses were hurt in any way.

THE OLIVER PLOW

The next time this large field was to be plowed, I coaxed Father into letting me use the riding plow. I pointed out that, as it plowed much wider sods, it would be faster.

He finally agreed, but only on condition that I plow it parallel to the road so that the difference in the width or look of the two sods made by this plow wouldn't show up as badly.

So I started plowing crosswise at the far end of the field, over eight hundred yards from the road. With four horses and my light weight, the horses could actually trot if they were so inclined. The long, gracefully curved mold-boards would lay the sods down perfectly.

At noon, after the horses were watered and were eating and I was resting against the dike in the sun, having eaten my meal, I looked up at the plow, which was almost over my head. I suddenly realized that I was looking at an adjustment at the back of the pole that the men had never known was there. I made a change with the aid of the old-fashioned wrenches in the toolbox and could hardly wait for the noon hour to be over.

At first the change I made wasn't all the answer. I had to backtrack a bit and change some other adjustments that had been tried before. However, before the day was over, I had it turning two identical sods.

Father drove by on his way to Tignish the next day. This time there was no sarcasm.

THRESHING

Back in those days, the harvesting of grain was done by binders. The day of the combine had not yet arrived. In fact, the days of the reapers were not long gone, although I had never seen a reaper in action myself.

Our neighbors, at least on one side, did not have a binder, so we did their work as well as the work on both of our farms.

The machinery was very well taken care of, especially by Father. If the binder was ever left out overnight, the canvasses were all removed and sheaves packed around the knotter and other parts.

We grew, on average, sixty acres of grain. Black oats were grown in that area of PEI. In fact, I didn't know there was any other kind until much later.

We also grew three acres of potatoes and about one-quarter of turnips. The potato and turnip land was sown in wheat the following year. The wheat provided us with flour, shorts (for porridge), middlings, and bran.

One year, when we had no hired man and a large crop of grain on the other farm, we were helped by a neighbor with his wagon and team, and his son. When we went into the large field to load, we were engaged in a friendly race to load. I pitched the sheaves on to Father, who built the load. Each load was to consist of the same number of stooks. In the case of the other team, the father threw on while the son built the load.

They were loaded and on the road ahead of us. However, we made a few unkind remarks about their load. As we followed them home, Father and I noticed their load shifting some. And sure enough, when they were crossing the bridge at Round Pond, which was a bit rough, about a dozen or more sheaves slipped off into the water.

So they admitted that they could have spent more time loading.

The grain was stored in the barn right out of the fields. What wouldn't go in the barn was stacked right outside the large barn doors.

The threshing in our district was done by Joe Smith, who had a portable rig. For the first years it was powered by a horse-powered treadmill. This mill was fitted with a pair of shafts and was backed up to the barn doors and blocked up to get the wheels off the ground. The mill, or thresher, had first been set up on the barn floor.

The treadmill was a two-horse affair, and Mr. Smith's horse was always used as one of them. We would put one of ours alongside of the Smith horse. However, our horse would tire quickly, and would have to change for a fresh one quite often. The Smith horse could go all day and never seemed to tire.

If the grain was damp and tough, the treadmill would be blocked up a bit higher in front. The large drive wheel to the thresher was equipped with a brake and operated by a rope and pulley arrangement, which was fastened close to Mr. Smith, who always fed the drum of the mill. If the supply of sheaves ran out for any reason, he only had to put the brake on and say whoa to the horses.

The threshing crew, about eight men all told, would be composed of neighbors and one or two men who more or less followed the rig.

Mother also arranged to have help for the two- or three-day job. The work in the barn was hard and the appetites large. Mother, in turn, would often help the women who helped her. This exchange of work applied through a great number of jobs.

The grain in our case was bagged and hauled by horse and cart to the granary. It came from the mill by a chute into a basket, and my job as a youngster was to tend and direct these into bags with twine from the sheaves.

Father loaded the bags into the cart and hauled them to the granary, which was a large area over the machine shed.

To get a little ahead of this story: During the milder days of winter and early spring, this grain, or a large part of it, had to be cleaned for seed, which was a large part of our cash crop. We (Father and I) would take turns filling or turning the "fanners." The clean oats were either bagged for sale or shoveled in an empty part of the granary. Before we really started, Father would set the various screens and air to what he thought was nearly right, run a small amount through and take a dishful into the kitchen, where he would spread it out on an opened newspaper on the table, in a good light. Then he would take a little three-legged magnifying glass and go all over the grain, searching for weed seeds.

Probably he would have to do this with several samples, changing sieves or their angle, or the air, before he was satisfied.

One day, when we had the crew and were threshing, Mother asked Mr. Smith to put Father's old felt hat through the mill. She was tired of seeing him wearing it. Sure enough, sometime in the afternoon when Father was stooping over the bag of grain, Smith grabbed the hat off his head and put it in ahead of a sheaf of oats. *Whoosh!* The hat made quite a noise going through the drum.

Giving Mr. Smith an awful look, Father went to the back of the cleaner and watched for the hat to come bobbing through. He grabbed it, gave it a couple of bangs over his knee to knock the straw and chaff off it, then put it on his head.

Of course it was in ribbons, but he wore it for the rest of the day.

If memory serves me right, Mother gave Mr. Smith a dollar to do this on a bet, a lot of money in those days.

LEMON PIE

One dinner, Mother served lemon pie for dessert. When one fellow was being served, his piece of pie accidentally tipped over his hand. Did he lose it? No, sir. Down went his knife between two fingers and up the other side, and his tongue neatly cleaned the pie from the knife. Then the next two fingers were scraped clean. He hadn't washed too well, if at all, and one side of the delicious pie was edged with black. The women started to laugh and couldn't get stopped. They were finally crying.

I forgot this man's name. However, the woman helping Mother was Amanda Leonard, a first cousin of hers.

SILVER BLACK FOXES

During our early years of living on the Kildare Cape, many of our friends and relatives were getting into the black fox business. Grandfather Rayner had been advising Father to start a ranch.

Breeding stock was then at its very highest. But finally, W. H Harding, our Greenmount minister, A. P. Wells, our next door neighbor and married to Mother's sister, and Father, joined together and built a ranch in a lovely spruce woods right behind our barn.

The care and feeding of the foxes was to be divided between the three men, with Father having the late-winter and spring months. This would put him in charge during the mating season and during the tricky time when the pups were being born.

Although the price paid for the original pair was so high (I have understood that the venture cost thirty thousand dollars), these men got out of it very well. The first litter of five pups sold so well that three of them took care of the debt, and two were put in as a second pair of breeders.

Of course, in those early days, one of the pups would be exchanged with someone in the same position, as brothers and sisters were not paired off.

The following autumn the crash in prices came, and we missed making a fortune by one year. With the care given by Father, though, and the terrific luck he had, they built the ranch up to fifteen or sixteen pair of breeders in a short time. He fed and cared for this ranch for eight years without having a pair miss and without losing a single pup, a record probably never equaled.

Father would allow no one, even of our family, around the ranch when pups were being born, and no noisy work, even around the barn. He talked continuously with the foxes, and a great many were quite tame.

In March of the ninth year, some ignorant person in an airplane buzzed the ranch and scared some of the female foxes, or vixens, so that they hid their young, some in burrows in the snow and some in the cold ground. Then began the frantic telephone calls to try to find a cat with kittens. Father found the pups in various places, apparently dead, and he brought them to the house in his warm hand inside his woolen mittens. Quite a few revived when placed on a warm cloth just inside the oven.

A cat with kittens would always adopt a young fox pup, and we raised quite a few in this manner when they were abandoned by their natural mothers. Our own cat was often pressed into this service, and one spring had raised seven pups from three separate litters for a friend of ours. She was fed on cream and eggs but even so, when we finally got her home she was very thin. Some of the oldest pups were still nursing from her when they were as large as she was.

***

When Christmas came around the following year, this man gave me an A. C. Gilbert Electrical set, which included parts for an electric motor. Both the field coils and the simple three-dash pole armature had to be wound by hand with the wire that was supplied.

I already had an erector set made by the same people and used Mother's old spinning wheel to power any models I made or put together.

Father watched me carefully winding and soldering and said that I was wasting time. "That thing will never run." We had our first Model T Ford then, but it didn't have a battery. So it was some time before I could show him that it certainly would.

Then the telephone man came and changed the dry cells in our phone. He not only gave me the old ones but checked a lot of other old ones he had and gave me a few of the best.

I connected four of them together and put two wires to the motor. It was a thrill to hear it humming along.

***

How did I get off the subject of foxes? Oh yes, because my cat had raised foxes for Pearly Haywood.

The ranches at first were built large. Each individual pen was thirty feet square. The sides were nine or ten feet high. The wire was dug two feet into the ground and had a two- or three-foot run on top of the ground and an overhang of about the same at the top. The first five feet and the two feet in the ground were of quite a heavy gauge. The upper part was not so heavy. The outside ranch that enclosed all the pens was built pretty much the same except that there was no wire dug into the ground.

The first fox house in our ranch was built to accommodate six families. Each apartment had a "kitchen" and a "den." The latter was a box about twenty inches in each dimension, built of two-ply groove and tongue boards, and was located in the kitchen. The chute from the pen was always built with an *L* in it to minimize draughts.

Then this apartment was enclosed in another big box that ran along each of the houses, with lots of room for shavings on the bottom and sides.

So our ranch was built at first to house six pair of foxes. It was doubled soon after, then again. These thirty-by-thirty-foot pens were divided by a double wire partition, and the extra pens were provided with single houses. It was later found that the animals didn't have to have contact with the ground, and the whole pen was raised a foot or so off the earth. This was cleaner and more healthy.

Father did his own skinning, cleaning, and stretching, and shipped his pelts to Lampson and Sons in London, England.

One year I included a few muskrat skins, a red squirrel, and a field mouse skin. This was a good year price-wise, and I received four dollars each for the muskrats, seventy-five for the squirrel and twenty-five for the mouse. Cents, that is.

The price paid by local buyers for muskrats that year was fifty cents and some buyers bought hundreds. The rats I sent were not large or of the best quality, and I imagine that the good ones brought over five dollars each.

Before leaving the subject of foxes, I will tell of the pets that sometimes resulted on raising them on a cat, one especially a fox pup called Bob.

We had a young collie pup the same year. Bob was allowed to run with the pup and they were great friends. They had the run of the farm, and I even took them with me to the other farm. They slept together under our back steps.

They came to the field with me up until the autumn, and would follow me up and down for a few rounds, then disappear to roam the woods on their own.

As Bob was now full grown, we were afraid he might be shot, so we had to put him in the large outside ranch, especially at night, as we never knew where they were in the evenings.

Uncle B. I. Rayner (for Benjamin Isaac) had a female fox that had also been raised on a cat. We traded another fox for her and paired the two tame ones. We called this female Bess. This pair raised many fine pups. In fact, the pelts from them brought the highest prices at the fur auction in London many times.

The amazing thing was that as soon as their first litter was born, Bob became snarly and cross, and protective of the pups. Bess, on the other hand, was forever tame and gentle. She was very proud of her pups and loved to have you pet and handle them.

Bess and Bob were eventually moved with the rest of the foxes to Charlottetown when we sold the farm and went there to live. But that move is another story.

Chapter 3

No excuse really to make a new chapter. This will be more of our life at Kildare Cape.

The farm there had a frontage on the shore of fifteen chains, or three hundred thirty yards. The cliffs below our farm were quite high, especially on the south side. On the north the cliffs were not so high, and we had access to the shore.

Always after a storm, Father or I would go down to the shore. Sometimes the storm would pile up a windrow of kelp, sometimes a windrow of gravel. In either case we would advise our neighbors, and if they had time they would come with a horse and cart to get a share of what was there.

Each farmer would have a pile of both kelp and gravel, which were added to when possible or when needed. The kelp was allowed to rot and was hauled to be mixed with manure for fertilizer.

The gravel was for concrete or to fill holes on the road or in the yard.

After one storm there was a lot of kelp. Father and I were the only ones interested. We had only loaded half a cart when we found a live lobster. And before noon we had a large number of them. We sure were lucky. They had become tangled in the kelp. We had never seen this before. And I guess we never did again.

There was a sandbar offshore about a hundred yards all along in front of our farm. A big storm would often change its position or the depth of water between it and the beach.

The "run" from the Round Pond would sometimes be sanded in after a storm. This pond was fed by three streams. When the run became closed, the pond would deepen until it broke out through the sand again. The beach below the pond was quite wide, and the run could change its course each time.

One of the streams flowing into this pond originated in a very fine spring on our property. This is where our cattle came to water through the winter months.

Our farmyard was almost completely surrounded by the woods or buildings, so the cattle would start off to the spring even in the worst storm. Sometimes, if the storm was bad, they would stop when they got down our lane a short distance and ran out of shelter. We might have to drive them a bit.

At the outer end the spring was also well sheltered, and sometimes the cattle would have to be encouraged to start for home. But most often the old bull would start, with the others following. The younger calves behind would have a good path broken for them. This all saved an awful lot of pumping. Once in a while, when the storm was too severe, we would water the cattle at the barn.

Before leaving the shore, I want to mention Aunt Carrie. She was Father's sister, and was married to Frank Treat. They lived in Hartford, as I mentioned earlier. They had one daughter, Betty, who is my only first cousin on Father's side of the family.

Aunt Carrie and Uncle Frank came to PEI on their honeymoon, and I think they came every summer of their married lives. Uncle Frank, who was an electrician, liked the out-of-doors, and would turn in and help with whatever job was being done.

They brought Betty as a baby, and each year as she got older. They all loved saltwater bathing, and Aunt Carrie was a terrific swimmer. Before we were old enough to swim alone she would take us on her back and "ferry" us out to the shallow water on the sandbar.

She could float as long as she had a notion to, and could even doze off to sleep when the water was calm.

Uncle Frank was a great storyteller and was great fun to have around. Years later, when Betty was married, we all went to her wedding and heard more of Uncle Frank's stories.

Cars were allowed to run on some roads, but only on certain days. The first were introduced in about 1914. A lot of horses were terrified, and some of the horse owners were worse. So at first they would only use the roads forbidden to autos, or go on the days that there would be no auto traffic.

We only had one horse that was a bit car shy. And this is how it happened. During a season between cropping and haying, when there wasn't much work for horses to do, all but one of ours were pastured in a large lower field. Each day, Father would hitch the one horse in the barn and take a bag of oats down to the field.

Just as he was about to do this one day, Uncle B. I. Rayner drove in with a new Baby Grand Chevrolet. He told Father to put the bag of oats in the car and he would take it down for us. The horses were all out of sight over the hill, so Father or I opened the gate and B. I. drove the car into the field. Then Dad called the horses. They came tearing over the hill, but all stopped when they saw the car. Father made a great show of pouring the oats into their individual boxes and placed them a short distance from the car. They soon came cautiously to the grain. As soon as they got into the oats, we took the boxes and set them on the wide running boards of the car.

While they were eating their oats, Uncle B. I. started the motor. They snorted and backed off, but soon came back. Then the car horn was blown, but they didn't pay much attention.

None of these four horses was a particle afraid of a car on the road from then on. The one left in the stable was afraid for a while, but gradually got used to cars too.

Some horses never did, but as I said, most of the fault was with the owner of the horse. One man in Greenmount by the name of Sellick had a fine animal, and always drove in a two-wheel sulky. When he saw a car approaching he would wheel around and go the other way until it passed. I guess he eventually got caught with a car coming from each direction and found the horse was not so afraid after all.

Frank, the horse of ours that was a bit shy of autos, was a peculiar one. He was raised by ourselves. He was large, always fat and shiny, and a very good worker. We usually used wheat straw for bedding, as it was considered to have little food value. But Frank would reach for every bit he could get at, and eat it before he would eat the choicest of hay.

We mostly left him unshod in the winter, as he was so good in deep snow. He would jump through it like a great jackrabbit, and seemed to enjoy it.

But above all the horses we ever raised, Lou was the best liked, and when we sold our stock at auction to move to Charlottetown, this little mare wasn't put on the block. In fact, Father drove Lou to Charlottetown. He had our hens in an enclosure in a light truck wagon, and Hunter, the collie dog that was a pup with Bob, our pet fox.

Hunter started off on the wagon but soon jumped off. So Father put a rope on him. He jumped off anyway and was caught and tied up shorter. But he jumped off again and would have hanged himself. So he was untied, and ran for miles. He started to lag and limp, so was taken into the wagon again. This time he was glad to stay.

They drove to Port Hill, where Dad had relatives with whom he stayed the night. Next day at 4:00 PM, they proudly drove into our new yard at Admiral Street in Charlottetown after a two-day drive of over 80 miles, and not on marvelous roads.

The Platts home on Admiral Street, Charlottetown

Lou never required any urging, but would trot as soon as one picked up the reins, and seemed keen to do so. However, leave her standing while you visited or shopped and she would never move. They don't come that way very often.

In Charlottetown, we lived on a street well down from the main road. There was one house below us, and Father told the mailman not to come so far just for our two families every day. There was a cedar post at the end of the street that had a split in it. So they made a plan that the daily paper and other mail could be left in the post. Father could see it from a living room window. Then he would jump on Lou's back and go out for it. Bridle or reins were not necessary because Father could depend on her to go and stop on his word, and she would turn away from his hand held out on either side.

If there was mail for the Thorns, Father would take it down.

My sister Emily was teaching in Cornwall and came home on weekends. One day there was a letter for her from Ottawa, and one for Father from Tignish. Father offered to trade with her. Emily only laughed at him. "You know what's in mine," she said. So Father opened his, and a one-thousand-dollar banknote was folded in the letter, the first and last one I ever saw. The DesRoche man who had purchased the other farm had sent it on account.

But Lou had brought me to Charlottetown before I was ready. So let's get back to Kildare Cape.

Round Pond was a fine place to fish, and trout were plentiful in those days. Uncle Al, whose farm was bounded on one side by this pond and the main stream flowing into it, was one fisherman. A bit greedy, perhaps, but very successful. He often caught more than they could use, so fed them to the foxes. There were no freezers in those days, and no limit on the fish you could take.

I caught a lot of trout, also. I had never fished with a fly. The reliable angleworms served me fairly well.

There would be runs of capelin each year also. Silversides is their proper name. Father made a contraption to use from the bridge, and one day we filled a carp box with them. Fine fox food.

Also, there would be a run of *gaspereaux* each spring to spoil our trout fishing. There was quite a large and deep hole in the upper end of the run from the pond to the sea. One year we put up a chicken wire fence across the run and when the hole filled with gaspereaux trying to get in we put another wire across the lower end. Then with dip nets, we filled the cart.

Father had the land ready for turnips, so he filled a drill with fish and then we went back for more. When we arrived home with the second load we found thousands of seagulls on the turnip land, and the gaspereaux pretty well gone. When he spread the second load he got the plow and closed the drill immediately.

ICESPERIENCE

One spring, a large iceberg came down from the north and grounded on the sandbar below our school. At noon hour one day, five or six of us went down to examine it.

There were about seventy-five yards of open water separating us from this great iceberg. The wind was on the shore. We got a couple of poles and used an ice cake to push ourselves out. I guess we were pretty excited. We sure weren't thinking right as we all climbed up to where we could see the school and a lot of the surrounding country.

It was so calm in the shelter of this great ice mass that we hadn't thought of our ice "boat" floating away. But when we went to return it had gone, with our poles, back to the shore. Were we ever in a mess! However, on the outside of the iceberg there was a lot of loose ice, and we found a piece that was large enough to carry a couple of us. After a lot of work, and without poles, we managed to get it around the grounded ice, and the wind took two of us to shore and we poled the large piece out for the others.

Of course we were late for school, and had a lot of explaining before we convinced the teacher that we hadn't meant to be.

The shore surely had attractions for each season. In the summer, a number of us boys often went in swimming. We didn't have swimsuits but would go around a point of rocky cliffs where the girls, who knew what was going on, wouldn't go beyond. Swimming was more or less frowned on, but I can't recall that this particular teacher had ever forbidden it.

However, one fine noon she and a couple of the older girls came down to the shore. They didn't come down on the beach but walked along up on the field until they were above where we were swimming.

We had to stay swimming in the deeper water until they left to go back. Then of course by the time we got dressed and back we were late for school.

Kind of a dirty trick!

I got a lot of time off school during the busy times on the farm. Often the teachers boarded with us and I got help at home. One year we had a third class teacher at school. So Father hired a real good first class teacher to live with us and teach several of us. Annie Matheson from Travellers' Rest was this teacher. My sister Emily also had a year at the convent in Tignish to help her education. Both she and Florence, my other sister, were attending Prince of Wales College in Charlottetown at an early age.

Chapter 4
OUR FIRST CARS

Around this time, about 1918, Father bought a Model T Ford and I soon learned to drive it. I had always been interested in mechanical things, especially if they ran on gasoline. We never had anything more complicated than a binder, with its ability to wrap up and tie a sheaf of grain. So I was pretty excited when Father was persuaded to buy a car. As far as I was concerned, the Model T was the first choice. It was to be my love through two of my Father's and one of my own.

These Model T Fords served us very well and would go as fast as roads would warrant.

There was no such thing as snow plows then, and the cars were put up on blocks through the winter months. We took the battery out of ours and stored it in the house. Once during winter it would be put in the car, the engine started by the crank, and allowed to run for an hour to put a charge into the battery.

The first battery had a wooden case and before the car was traded for another, the case rotted out. There was a large circus coming to Summerside and I wanted to go. The girls put the pressure on Father. He finally agreed for us to have the car on circus day, but I had to agree to have a new battery box put on. We both thought the car would have to be put in the garage in Summerside while this was being done.

So off we went. We took our two cousins, Irene and Grace Wells, and our three selves. On the way down, steam started to fly from the radiator and we found a broken fan belt. We drove into a barnyard and were able to make one from a piece of leather strap, which did nicely until we were able to buy a new one in Summerside.

And at Taylor and Macneill's, Mr. Taylor removed the battery and grounded the generator, so we were able to use the car all day.

All I had to do was start it by the crank, which dangled in place at all times, and go back to the garage before dark.

When we picked up the battery, which looked like brand-new, we were agreeably surprised. It only cost one dollar. And for good measure, Mr. Taylor played us several beautiful tunes on an ordinary hand saw. He did this by two methods, by tapping and with a violin bow.

With the money I saved I bought a "Bulldog" foot accelerator and installed it myself. Father wouldn't use this improvement, but continued to use the hand throttle on the steering column. The next Model T was factory equipped with exactly the same kind of foot accelerator. So this time he used it.

Some time after this, Father decided we would paint the car, as it was getting kind of shabby-looking. He bought a quart of real fine enamel and lots of sandpaper. We sanded and cleaned all one afternoon and by late afternoon or early evening had it ready for painting.

We decided to put the car in a grassy field on the sunny side of a quiet bush, and we went at it with a new brush each. We made a very fine job of it, too.

We left it to dry for the rest of the evening. A bit before dark, Father went and brought it home. It looked an awful mess. The black flies had got into the paint before it was dry. We were all feeling pretty bad that night. The paint wasn't dry enough to do anything about the insects that night so we put the car in the garage and shut the door.

When the car was washed with a cloth and cold water the next day the flies came off pretty well and it looked fine. No one ever noticed anything wrong with the paint job.

Mother occasionally drove our car, and one day as we were returning from Alberton, we saw some farmers using a hay loader. None of us had ever seen one before. While we all had our eyes on the man, Mother drove around a sandy corner at South Kildare. The steering gear went hard over and stayed that way. The car went across a shallow ditch, up a small dike, and stalled against a fence. Father said, "If you want a closer look, you'll have to walk." We all had a good laugh, and no harm done.

The longest trip we children made alone was to New Glasgow to a church convention. We stayed with the Dickensons, Alder, Ritchie, and Ruth, for the weekend. They drove a 490 Chevrolet.

It was a rainy Sunday, and when we went home from church in their car they couldn't get up their lane, which was quite steep and slippery. We left their car on the road and used the Model T, which went up the lane okay. I was sure proud.

These were very fine people.

This trip from Kildare Capes to New Glasgow and return was considered a long one in those days.

Weekly ballgames were held around among our friends. A suitable pasture field would be selected. There were no spectators; everyone played, right down to the smallest children. Potato bags partially filled with sand were used as bases and to mark the pitcher's mound. There was no such thing as "three out, all out." Everyone had a turn at the bat.

And if you "offered" and the catcher caught the ball, you were out.

The balls were made of yarn and the bats were homemade. Lunch was always served, mostly inside after darkness stopped the game. With the advent of the automobile, the games could start earlier. Those with horses who came late would be chosen by the captains and they took their turn at bat or in the field, or a good pitcher could pitch for the team he was chosen to be on.

Uncle Archie had a Briscoe, and we could tell when he was coming for quite a while before he arrived with his large family.

Uncle Jim had a very large six-cylinder Overland that had a cut-out in the exhaust pipe ahead of the muffler. It was operated by a step-on gadget and if he wanted to advertise his coming he could use this rig, which sure gave the car a distinctive roar, especially on a hill. Dan Getson had a Grey Dort, and Perley and Ed had a Model T, as did Boyd Hammell and his parents.

One time we had a dressmaker at the house for a few days. Father was continually teasing her. One day she sat at the sewing machine that she and Mother had pulled into a bay window between the kitchen table and the wash stand. Father had pulled a chair up behind and to one side of her. She suddenly turned and gave him a slap across the face.

She immediately got a few shades of red as she blushed and apologized. Apparently a kitten playing on the floor had jumped at something around her leg as she worked the treadle of the machine. When she saw right away that it couldn't possibly have been Father, she became very embarrassed. And he sure had a great laugh at her.

You may have forgotten about it, but I eventually did get the .22 caliber rifle, a Stevens Little Scout—a single-shot model, and probably one of the best ever produced, and quite inexpensive too. I forget the cost but believe it was four dollars and seventy-five cents.

Father also acquired a twelve-gauge double-barreled shotgun at about this time, but I never knew of him going hunting. He enjoyed going to parties at Perley Heywood's, where they used BB caps to shoot targets in the basement. In fact, he brought some pretty fine targets home to boast about.

One day when I wasn't home, he rushed into the house, grabbed my rifle and asked Mother to find him some ammunition. She could only find two bullets. He said he had seen a partridge in the woods. Mother told him to take the shotgun. "No," he said. "Anyone can shoot a partridge with a shotgun, and probably ruin it for eating."

Very soon after he came in with two fine native grouse, both shot cleanly through the head.

I really think the reason he didn't take the twelve-gauge was that he was a bit afraid of it.

When Uncle E. H. Rayner would visit us occasionally, he would want a fowl for dinner. And he always wanted to shoot it. I would catch a "ducker" and carry her, or probably a "spare" rooster, up to the door in the granary. I would throw the poor bird as high as I could out over the barnyard.

Uncle E. H. would insist that Herb would shoot first, which only meant that I would often have to catch the luckless bird and repeat the performance, when E. H. would skillfully dispatch the flying hen or rooster. E. H. said that Father always shut both eyes just before he pulled the trigger.

Like Uncle Frank Treat, Uncle E. H. always had a good story for every occasion and we always enjoyed his visits. Another visitor we always enjoyed was "Professor" Walter Shaw, a cousin of Father's. Walter was getting an education, and much later he became premier of our fair island. The term *professor* was more of Father's teasing.

To get back to guns again: it wasn't long before I was using the twelve-gauge and bringing home some ducks for the table. I liked hunting, and always went somewhere on the opening day of the duck season. Never missed after I became old enough until our wedding day, which happened to fall on the first day of the hunting season.

So you can realize that the writer didn't have much to do with making the wedding plans.

***

The job of picking wild strawberries was not liked by any of us. However, we made a competitive game of it, and generally got along very well.

Being the eldest, I could naturally pick as many or more berries than my sisters. However, one day Florence had her dish full quicker than either Emily or I. When Mother emptied them into a stewing dish she found that Florence had a three- or four-inch layer of grass in the bottom of her basket!

We could buy lovely looking buckets of wild berries from our French neighbors who lived in the Cock Road. However, we had watched them pick and didn't like the way they hulled the berries. They hulled them with their mouths, putting the berries in on one side and out the other into their container, and the hulls out the front. They could pick very fast.

After Father bought a car, we often went on some wonderful berry-picking picnics. I especially remember a trip to Mary and Herbert Alley's in Alma, or maybe it was Elmsdale. At one time there had been a millpond below their home. The dam had let go and there was only a nice stream with high banks on each side. The banks had grown up in raspberry canes. And were they ever loaded! You could pick at nearly eye level and could fill a pail very quickly.

Another trip for wild strawberries was to a field in Montrose. Uncle Jim Rayner and some of his family were there. I don't recall that Uncle Jim picked berries himself, but when a rabbit ventured out of the woods coming on evening, James pulled a revolver from a holster under his left arm and took two shots at the bunny before it reached the safety of the woods.

The Alleys mentioned earlier were a queer pair. Herbert was a meek intellectual, Mary was all gab. She had a beautiful horse and was well set up with a fine, wire-wheel driving wagon for use in summer and a "Francis" sleigh for winter travel.

And travel she did. She sold some expensive brand of corsets and roamed far and wide. She put up at various homes through the country and stayed overnight at our house once in a while.

One winter evening she arrived, and after giving Father and me explicit instructions on the stabling and care of the horse, she took herself and her sample case into the house.

Before we had a furnace we used a base burner in the living room and an "Air Tight Hummer" in the dining room. This day, Mary had on an expensive fur coat, which she took off and draped over a high-back dining room chair on her way through to the living room, and thence on through it to the spare bedroom.

Mother had given the threaded draft a twist open as she passed the stove. They were quite a while in the other end of the house and when they came back the Hummer and stovepipe above it were red-hot, and the coat was scorched badly.

This lady didn't get along very well with her husband. One time she confided to Mother, "I only hit Herbert once in my life. I hit him over the head with a dishpan, and I put it right down to his shoulders."

I lost track of this couple when we moved to Charlottetown.

The stovepipe from this Hummer went out through the ceiling in the dining room. Father had bought and installed a heat-saving device to get heat back before it entered the flue. Actually, it was a sheet iron unit somewhat larger than the Hummer itself.

The room above was as large as the dining room below and when there was a fire in the Hummer, it was quite comfortable.

It was my room except when there was a teacher staying with us. Then I was moved to a smaller bedroom. Before the hot air furnace was put in we always had a base burner in the living room in the winter. This lovely unit burned hard coal in an amount that would maintain a fire overnight. The design had mica windows in all the doors and was beautiful to see in the morning. I would always gather up my clothes and run down and dress alongside this stove in the winter mornings. Father would have been down, shaken it up, and opened the drafts.

One morning there was a large clothes basket on two kitchen chairs alongside the glowing stove. There was a blanket draped over the basket. When I raised the blanket there were about a dozen little pink pigs. A more beautiful sight it would be hard to imagine. Mother, to her dying day, always maintained that the only thing more beautiful was a small baby's feet. Father, who had been up with the old mother pig, probably thought these little fellows were pretty nice also. He surely spent a lot of time with young foals, lambs, calves, and pigs.

We had a very lovely garden area, sheltered on three sides by the heavy spruce woods but exposed on the south and with a gentle slope in that direction. About half the area was given over to early potatoes. There were many rows of beans, most all for baking. And each of us three children had a plot of our own to care for from planting to harvest, as well as doing our share in weeding the larger garden. The baking beans gave us a few pleasant evenings in the winter as one of us read out loud, mostly Florence, while the others shelled the beans. We had an empty sugar barrel and would fill it with the dry beans. Then I would get in the barrel and jump around for quite a while. Then each one would take a share of the beans from the barrel and go over them for the odd pod that might have a bean or more in it. When this bunch was done, the barrel would be filled again.

We all read a great deal. I read every Alger book ever written, and the girls read books of interest to them—Elsie Dinsmore and Ruth Fielding books, etc. Also all the books and magazines we could get our hands on.

Back to the garden: Father grew some fine celery with wide boards staked up on each side of the plants. We also put up a barrel of sauerkraut each winter. Our Dutch friend, Dan Getson, had made himself a fine plane for cutting cabbage, which he gladly loaned to us. This cutter had a box to hold the cabbage. The box slid in grooves across an old scythe blade in a plank, which was supported on the barrel to be filled. The blade was adjustable so the cabbage could be cut fine or coarse. This sauerkraut sure was good when cooked up with a piece of pork from the barrel of pork we also put up every year (as well as a barrel of beef). Mother's jam shelf was large and well stocked. Berries were plentiful, and the garden products supplied a quantity of fruit, pickles, etc. We had apples, cherries, pears, and two of the most beautiful damson plum trees I have ever seen.

THE MILL POND

Father made frequent trips to a grist mill handy to Alberton, which was at that time owned by Johnston Heywood, who was a cousin of his. Later this mill was run by a Rix, but it has long since ceased to exist. We had oats to be crushed and wheat to be ground. Sometimes Father would go early in the day and stay until the grain was processed. One morning he agreed to take me and we would fish while we waited for the grist. When we were digging for worms in Johnston's garden, we found a huge one. Too large for bait, we agreed, but we took it anyway.

We fished from a raft which we poled around. We caught no trout for some time but lost all our worms to minnows, which nibbled our hooks bare. We were down to this large worm, which we cut in sections and shared. We found a good spot, an old stump, and caught a fine string of trout, all with pieces of the one worm.

The grist mill, to me at that age, was a mechanical marvel. It was run by a huge water wheel. The gears were large and had renewable teeth of hardwood. The grinding was by stones. The miller took a "toll," so no money was involved unless a customer wanted to purchase additional products.

Many years later, when we lived in Charlottetown, a couple of friends and my brother-in-law, Bob MacNeill, drove up to the stream at the head of this pond to fish. Bob hooked a fine trout but his trailing fly got hooked in an alder root at the bottom of a deep hole. He called to me and we could see no way to get the fish, which was now tethered at the bottom in plain sight. Bob was for trying to pull the line until something broke in the hope that it would be the hook that was caught.

I said just a minute, and I took off my clothes and dove down and unhooked the line from the root. Then Bob landed his fish while I dressed. So all in all, this mill has a mixture of memories. It has gone the way of a great many such mills. To the best of my knowledge, as I write this in 1976, there is only one grist mill currently in operation on P. E. Island. This is Laird's Mill in Coleman, which we patronize frequently. And this mill now uses a Cat diesel engine for power. Mr. Laird found the water not reliable enough. Continuous clearing of the forests has let the springs that helped to fill the millponds dry up. Such is progress. Belle buys island flour, shorts, middlings, bran, whole wheat cereal, a doctor's mixture, and cream of wheat, called wheat germ by Mr. Laird.

When I was old enough to have a driver's license, I began to take in the dances around the country. I was very fortunate to have the company of a former school friend who was a couple of years my senior and who loved to dance as much as I did. Probably the fact that I had the use of my Father's car influenced her acceptance of my company. However, we certainly had some good times.

The square dances were the "in" thing then, and the music a fiddle and a piano. We were often the first couple on the floor. Mary was very popular, though, and I had plenty of competition. "Basket suppers" were a means for church and other organizations to raise money, and the fancy decorated baskets of lunch were smuggled into the hall under cover so that quite often the bidder wouldn't be sure of whose basket he was trying to buy when they were being auctioned. Sometimes we were given a clue. The successful bidder ate lunch with the basket's owner. These were indeed fine evenings. My sisters were soon old enough to go to dances also. Florence was considered one of the best piano players for square dances, so was in great demand. There were other fine pianists, though, so she got her turn on the dance floor too. Helen Dunbar, who later married my cousin George Rayner, was definitely the best pianist. Both she and Florence always watched the "sets" and adjusted the tempo of the music to the various parts of the dances.

Chapter 5

LEAVING THE FARM

The autumn of 1920 found me in Charlottetown to take a course in motor mechanics. This school was in what had been the Rena MacLean Memorial Hospital. After World War One, this building, together with the Government House, was converted and used as an agricultural college. Motor mechanics, carpentry, and blacksmithing were also taught, and I took these three courses.

Ralph Rayner accompanied me that winter. Before Christmas, we boarded on Kent Street over an oyster bar run by a Carver. After Christmas, we were at a Mrs. MacEachern's on Richmond Street.

Ralph and I competed for the attention of Mrs. MacEachern's daughter, Marjorie, for high marks at school, and for "spoons" in rifle shooting at the armory. Ralph won the spoons.

The MacEacherns set a wonderful table, and their place made a popular eating spot for the farmers from across the harbor who travelled the ice in the winter. These people often brought produce for sale: split firewood, grain, vegetables, etc., and took coal, groceries, and other purchases home. By noon they would often be well fortified for the cold trip home.

One noon, Ralph saw a fellow go into the bathroom with a bottle and come out without it. He found the Teddy bottle in the tall water pitcher with a towel draped over it. This was a kind of decorative arrangement, and the fellow considered it a good hiding place. To save the poor chap from intoxication and perhaps getting lost on the ice on his way home, Ralph took charge of the bottle and hid it in our bedroom.

I had never tasted rum and I don't suppose Ralph had either, but that evening as we were going down to the shower room at the school gymnasium, we each took a couple of drinks of the lovely stuff.

Our habit was to quite often take a couple of towels and a change of underwear and have a workout in the gym, followed by a hot shower. This particular evening was quite cold, but we scarcely noticed this. But by the time we got under the hot shower we commenced to get kind of silly. We were alone, and in adjacent shower stalls. We tried to scald or chill each other by opening or closing the hot or cold water in our own shower in an effort to change the temperature in the other one. We soon had the room full of steam and found ourselves off our feet and on the cool floor at the other end of the room.

Someone came in and closed the two hot water faucets or valves. We eventually got dressed and out into the cool night.

We were amazed at the power of the stuff and shook hands on our mutual promise to drink no more of it.

Whatever happened I never found out, but the next day at noon Ralph was late for dinner. And when he did come he was very drunk! He came to the table and sat a while, looking at his plate. The fork skidded, and much of his dinner went overboard onto the table and his lap.

Marjorie and I helped him upstairs and into bed, where he spent the afternoon. I never saw him drink again.

We had some wonderful teachers for the various courses at this school. A Mr. Campbell, an Old Country Scotchman, was our blacksmith instructor, and he taught us the basics of the forge. We made things of iron and steel we could take home, such as "S" hooks and clevis pins, cold chisels, pin punches, etc. In later years, when I worked at Bruce Stewart & Co. a machinist, Joshua Barnes offered me a dollar for a cold chisel after having borrowed and used it a while. A chisel this size was normally worth fifteen cents in those days, or perhaps twenty-five.

For carpentry we had a Mr. Waugh, and our motor mechanics teacher was Harry Whitlock, a good mechanic who was very fussy about cleanliness.

Also we had a driver's course. I was the student with most experience with the Model T so I was made an assistant instructor! Ralph had a lot of experience with other cars so he had the gear shift bunch. Roads and cross streets were laid off in the harbor ice and four or five students per car were taken out on fine afternoons to take their turn at the wheel. I had my turn at the wheel of the car with the standard transmission but, as this was entirely new to me, I was pretty clumsy.

All in all this proved to be a fine way to spend a winter, and a lot of things learned at the impressionable age of fifteen were never forgotten. I passed the motor mechanics course second to Hollis Moore and he was doing it as a repeat year, having failed the course in 1919.

Next year, in 1921, I really set my sights high and went to the Sweeney Auto School in Kansas City, Missouri. After a very long train trip I was quickly enrolled as #2364 and was just as quickly persuaded to buy a twenty-five-dollar book of meal tickets to their cafeteria and a large safety pin with five tokens on it stamped with my new number.

I shortly found a fine rooming house quite close to the school. I shared a room with three other fellows, all strangers to each other: two double beds in the room, and my bedfellow was Carl Yohnke from Toledo, Ohio. The two others shared the second bed.

We four were very lucky, as we all got along extremely well and enjoyed our stay together. We ate at the school cafeteria or at some nearby restaurant, and went to an occasional movie.

However, most of our evenings were spent in our room, reading, studying, or playing cards. After such a quiet evening we would frequently go out for a bite to eat. Sometimes we would all go, sometimes two of us, and quite often just one would go: the others would put up the money and the active one would bring back hot dogs and pop, ice cream or whatever.

One night, New Year's Eve 1922, Carl elected to go for the eats. He left just after eleven but he failed to return. We three waited and waited, then began to worry.

We finally decided to go out and look for him. The rooming house was up on a high hill and to get down to the school and stores, etc., we used a shortcut path that went around an old abandoned rock quarry. Two of us went by this path down to the lunch and hot dog stand we usually patronized, where we were told that Carl had indeed been there but had gone some time before.

Thinking that he may have returned by the long way, we went back. But no, he still hadn't returned. So two of us decided to search the quarry. We had never been around in the jumble of bushes, weeds, old machinery, sheds, and garbage, not even in daylight. Certainly not at midnight on a moonless night. Ken, the second searcher, went along the regular path to come into the quarry from the far end. I went in from the street end at the top. We were to meet at the back or deepest part of the hole, which was right under the path.

We didn't even have a flashlight. As I felt my way along, at my very feet there were two quick thumps, then the sound of something running: a rabbit. When my heart stopped hammering, I decided to look into an old shed off a bit to one side. The door was closed but there was a latch. I opened it and went feeling my way around in the pitch-black darkness, with my arms out and shuffling my feet along, half-expecting to find a human body (Carl's?) which some robber had hidden in there. My exploring hands and arms ran along a roost on which some hens were or had been sleeping. This time I nearly died when the hens squawked!

I thought it was of no use to look further in there as the chickens would not have been so quietly sleeping if they had recently been disturbed. So I backed out and went on in the quarry until I met Ken. We went up to our room again.

Carl had returned just before we arrived. When they heard us coming, Carl hid in a closet and the fellow we had left in the room tried to look and act as worried as when we left. However, he couldn't keep a straight face, so Ken and I knew that Carl was OK.

Where had Carl been? He had heard horns, music, and bells, and seen fireworks, so had gone over the bridge into Kansas to watch. We didn't appreciate the cold dogs or the warm pop.

I mentioned the ten-dollar safety pin on which were the five discs. These discs were for a deposit on tools taken from the school store, and were worth two dollars each. A small tool, such as a screwdriver or a pair of pliers, was obtained by depositing one disc. A valve grinder or other larger tool took all five. When the tool was returned, so was your disc. When you left the school and returned the pin you were refunded your ten dollars, less two for each missing numbered disc! A very fair method, we thought.

Now about the book of meal tickets: I loved rabbit, as we ate them occasionally at home. So at first I appreciated the dinners, but soon found that I didn't like rabbit all that well. It was served almost daily, and more often than once most days. Fried rabbit, roast rabbit, rabbit stew, rabbit pie, and rabbit soup.

So one day after about a week I went across the square to the large railway station, watched for a green-looking boy to get off the train, and asked him if he was going to Sweeney's. Yes, he was. So I persuaded him to buy the rest of my meal tickets at a discount. I explained that he would be pressured to buy one when he enrolled. But if he had a book of tickets he would get by. I explained about the rabbit. He assured me that he liked rabbit. I never saw this boy again. He would be in a class a week or so behind me and I seldom went to the cafeteria after that.

Carl Yohnke was a fine chap, and he persuaded me to accompany him to his home in Toledo, Ohio, when we both graduated without having to repeat any classes.

I liked his family and we both got jobs on the Pennsylvania Railway as machinist helpers. The shop was on strike and we were classed as scabs. However, the pay was good, and with lots of overtime we soon saved enough to repay the money we had borrowed to go to Sweeney's.

We worked a middle shift, going to work at 3:30 p.m. and coming off at midnight. No time for movies or social activities. So what money we earned was mostly saved.

Carl owned an ancient Model T Ford that we worked on during the forenoons. This car was a right-hand drive one but we changed it over to left. This necessitated a new transmission cover and some changes in the steering parts. Everything was carefully overhauled as we went. There was no starter or battery other than a six-volt dry cell for easier starting. The coil box had a push button combination lock. I thought I would never forget the combination but I have. It had kerosene side lights, a brass radiator shell and a very high fold-down windshield. We enjoyed working on it and future use proved that we did a good job.

At the railway shop we were both soon doing machinist jobs, while the machinists played cards in some washroom or hidden in a locomotive cab. When our mates on the next shift failed to show up, either one or the other or occasionally both of us would work through until morning. Then once in a while, the helper on the morning shift wouldn't show up either and we worked the third shift. The second shift we would be on time and a half, and the third on double time.

We both worked hard and loved it. We won the respect and confidence of the machinist inspector and after he had inspected a locomotive, if he couldn't find a machinist he would give the RRS (Running Repair Sheet) to one of us. We would do the work on our own before hunting up our machinist to sign the sheet before passing it back to the inspector, who would check that the work had been done right.

There was a lot of very fine singing in the large roundhouse. There might be as many as eight men at work on adjacent engines. The hostler and grease monkey on our shift were both colored men, and my machinist for a few weeks, a fellow by the name of Tippy, was as fine a tenor as I have ever heard. Both the Negroes had wonderful bass voices. Carl and I could carry a tune but not much more. So we would help to get them started and then just listen.

The hostler would sing from the locomotive cab, where his job was to get up steam on a cold engine. The grease monkey would be in the pit with his head out between the wheels when the singing got good. Even the shift foreman never said a word when Tippy and the boys got together on a song.

These "scab" machinists would often get a fortnight's pay, or at best a month's, and then not be seen again. Tippy stayed around longer than most. He was quite elderly, and had many interesting stories to tell. He had worked for some time in South America and had worked with a party building a rail line through Venezuela. One day the cook served them a fine dinner of steaks of delicious white meat. He wouldn't tell the men what it was until after dinner. Then he told them it was boa constrictor. No one objected, he said, and they had it often as they worked the line through the jungle.

One evening we heard a loud crash and we all rushed out to see a large engine in the turntable pit. A hostler had kindled a fire in a cold engine in the yard and had not checked to see that the throttle and other levers were closed or in the neutral position. When the boiler got hot and started to make steam the engine silently backed into the pit!

We had the pleasure of seeing a mighty crane and working crew lift it bodily and set it on the rails.

On another evening when we went to work we found the brick wall of the roundhouse in front of one set of tracks completely demolished. They had brought a locomotive in off the road with one side out of order. They had moved it across the turntable and almost into the roundhouse, with one piston only. Before it was quite far enough this piston stopped "on center." As the hostler worked the throttle, a workman jacked the engine ahead with a hand jack. Suddenly the crankshaft got past the dead spot and the thing jumped ahead and through the wall.

This Pennsylvania line had some of the fastest passenger locomotives ever built. Also some of the mightiest freight ones. The drivers on the fast passenger engines were so large in diameter that I could just barely reach to their top. And the powerful freight engines would just go on the turntable with an inch to spare. It was thrilling to me to work on such monsters.

Carl and I were planning to drive the Model T to Prince Edward Island in the spring, and through April our feet were getting itchy. The weather was so lovely in Toledo and the car was ready to go. We were getting kind of fed up on so much overtime and we decided one day to turn thumbs down on any more.

A few evenings later I was asked by the foreman if I would work the next shift. I said no thank you. Then he asked Carl, who said he didn't feel like it either. One word led to another and the foreman said he would have us fired if we refused to work. We told him to go ahead. He started to go toward the office. I looked out a back door and saw that the track of the turntable was lined up with the office. So we walked across it and into the office and asked for our time.

The foreman then blustered in and said, "I want those boys fired!"

"That's impossible," said the timekeeper. "They just quit."

So, on the first day of May 1922, we headed for PEI. We had a very fine trip. Slept in barns, church horse stables, and under the car astraddle a depression up a mountain. This was somewhere along the Erie Canal system. We fed ourselves and never once went into a restaurant. The weather was beautiful and we surely had a very fine trip of it. We put pound cans of beans on the exhaust manifold of the car after punching a couple of holes in the top. This would be done a half-hour or so before we planned to eat. However, when we tried to buy this size can of beans in Maine stores we found they were not stocked. Five pounds was the smallest. So we were off beans for a while.

The kerosene lamps on the cowl of the car were held on their bracket by a set screw, and very easily removed for use as lamps in the center of our eating table, or placed on a stump.

One night we stopped and asked permission to sleep in a fine barn, as it was a cold evening. The man was nice enough but said a firm no. He didn't want his barn burned down. We assured him that neither of us smoked, which was true, but he stuck to his no.

We drove down the highway a short distance, turned off on a side road and saw another fine, large barn with large double doors. We drove up, opened the doors, drove the car right in and quickly closed the doors again. We had been quick and quiet but still supposed that someone had seen us. As far as we could tell, this barn was on the farm of the man who had turned us down. We took our rugs and blankets up into the hayloft and had a fine night, but left before we ate breakfast in the morning. We often did this, as it divided up the day better.

One day, on a particularly rough road, we were following a Model T roadster that had a bit of a trunk arrangement at the rear. The cover of this wasn't fastened and when it bounced up we could see parcels bouncing inside. After a while a loaf of bread fell out, which we retrieved and quickly overtook the car again. Then a loaf of buns fell out. We intended to catch up again and return the groceries but they turned off onto a side road before we caught them.

As we crossed Lake Champlain on a ferry, we talked to a chap on a motorcycle whom we had seen several times before, and on different days. We were apparently making as good time as he.

Along the Erie Canal, which our route followed for a long distance, we were puzzled as to where we would spend the night. A railway paralleled us to the left and the canal to our right. Then we saw a gap in the railway fence and a trail up the mountain. We crossed the track and drove up the mountain until the fuel refused to feed the engine. Then Carl cut the wheel and backed by gravity over a nice, grassy depression in the ground. We had a hot supper and spent a cozy night under the car.

On still another evening we drove behind a church where there was a long horse shed. The top, back, and sides were covered. The wind was from behind so it was comfortable. We scraped some hay together, spread our rugs and spent a very fine night.

When we arrived at the border at St. Stephen, we were informed that all the bridges across the St. John River were washed out, including the railway one. There had been a large snowfall that winter and a sudden thaw in the first days of May had caused heavy flooding. A temporary railway bridge was being built but all roads were impassable. So we went back to Calais where we found a fine, low-cost place to leave the car, and next day we took the train for Tignish.

We had not told my folks that we were coming so when we arrived at Tignish at around nine in the evening of May the seventh, we started to walk the three or more miles to my home. Carl had brought a very heavy rifle he owned and we each carried a heavy suitcase. The roads were horrible; banks of snow on each side and mud in between. A good moon and clear sky, however.

Our house was in a woods about two hundred fifty yards from the road so when we got closer we took off across the field. When we came to our lane the snow was so deep that we were able to step over the telephone wires! This was surely something for Carl to write home about.

The doors were not locked. I don't think there was any means of locking them. So we walked right in, mud and all, and upstairs. I said "Hello!" Someone said, "Everett!" and Florence jumped out of bed and grabbed Carl with a big embrace. So I guess he felt welcomed.

Carl stayed with us all summer, working here and there, as did I, and we had a fine time. On Dominion Day, July first, we made a freezer of ice cream, frozen with snow and ice in the woods. There was some ice left, which we covered with spruce boughs and made another batch on the Fourth of July for our American friend, something more for him to write home about.

Father and Mother, especially Mother, were getting tired of farm work. We never had a tractor or other power. We used kerosene or

Coleman lights and we three children were ready to get out on our own. I was not interested in running a farm.

So Father bought a house in Charlottetown with seven acres of land and was making arrangements to build a fox ranch in the fairly large apple orchard. We had an auction sale. The driving sleigh with which Father courted Mother brought a higher price than he had paid for it. Also, our binder that had cut three and sometimes four crops each season was sold for much more than the original cost. As noted earlier, he didn't sell Lou, our driving mare, but drove her to Charlottetown.

Carl and Ralph Rayner went out west on the "harvest excursion" that autumn. They came back to Calais, picked up Carl's Model T and drove to Worcester, where they went to work in a wire mill.

Shortly after we had moved to Charlottetown, Ralph phoned from Worcester that I was sure to get a job there if I were to go at once. So I went, and got a job.

The boys were working by piecework, which I maintain is the way all work should be carried on if at all possible. I was broken in on a loom new to that mill. By Christmas they were getting so far ahead of sales that some of us were laid off.

So I got a job carrying for a brick mason who was building a flue in a new house. When the chimney was finished, the contractor gave me a job with him. He had five other houses finished but not sold. When that house was completed he had no further work for me, so I went home.

While in Worcester, we three (Carl, Ralph, and I) had some fine times. We had adjoining bedrooms and asked the landlady if we could move all the beds into one room and use the other room as a living room. There was a door between. She went along with us but stipulated that we couldn't have any women in our rooms. If we did, "Out you go," she said.

One day, Ralph's sister, Mary, and another cousin arrived in Worcester and landed noisily at our quarters. Soon the landlady knocked and called me into the hall. I took her in and introduced her. She was satisfied and the sparks stopped flying. Carl and Mary were later to become husband and wife. They had been keeping company on PEI.

We found a bakery where we could buy wonderful pies on Monday mornings at a very low price. My favorite was raisin, and Ralph preferred creamy ones. We would exchange a quarter, then eat a pie each!

We also patronized a fellow who brought oranges in from Florida in a paper-lined boxcar, and who sold them right out of the car. The ungraded ones were fifty cents for a large shopping bag, about a half-bushel. Some were small but a lot of them were as large as grapefruit. So we were never out of oranges.

As Ralph and Carl worked a night shift and I worked by day, we didn't see very much of each other except for weekends. I found a picture theatre that featured vaudeville and animal acts between movie shows. Once they had a bunch of trained seals. Half were dressed in red uniforms and the rest in green. And the stage was laid out as a baseball diamond. They took their positions and played by tossing a fairly large ball back and forth on their noses. The "man" at bat would flop to first base when he hit the ball. If a fielder got the ball he would toss it to his teammate on first base and if he got it before the "runner" got there he was out, and would retire to the side. They seemed to know all the rules of the game. There were other animal acts that were pretty amazing to a young country boy.

As I said, I went back to PEI shortly after the new year. I soon got a job at Bruce Stewart's garage. I lived at home. I bought myself a bicycle for summer transportation but walked to and from work in the winters. My weekly salary at garage work was six dollars!

However, I thoroughly enjoyed my work. The garage foreman was Percy Acorn. Bruce Stewart was a gruff but kindly elderly man. He owned a large six-cylinder Overland. It was the same model as one my Uncle Jim Rayner had. Frank Stewart, a lesser member of the firm, had a quite large four-cylinder Overland and C. L. MacKay, a senior executive, owned a Model Ninety. When work was scarce in wintertime we were often occupied by overhauling these cars. The large six-cylinder engine in Mr. Bruce Stewart's car was a Continental. This beautiful motor did not have a removable cylinder head. Rather, it had removable plugs over each valve.

One job we did on a number of older cars was to remove the body and cut out all the rivets with which the frames, running board and fender bracket, engine mounts, etc. were put together, and replace them with hot rivets, or if the rivet holes were worn badly, to ream them out and use bolts and lock-washers to refasten all parts.

I was no good as a striker, so my job was to hold the long chisel for Percy, who was fairly good with the sledge. Occasionally Frank Stewart, if he knew what was going on, would drop down from the machine shop, doff his coat, roll up the sleeves of his white shirt and wield the sledge for a while with either Percy or me holding the chisel. You could hold the latter, which was about two feet long, with the thumbs and fingers of your hands and not feel a jar, it being hit so squarely. Jerry Jackson, an old blacksmith turned machinist, was also a perfect striker.

One Monday morning, Frank Stewart drove his large four-cylinder car into the garage and told us to remove the oil pan and put new inserts in the big end of the number three connecting rod. As the motor was running quietly, we thought he must be fooling. He assured us that he was serious so we went to work at it.

These cars had a "mud pan" that extended from frame to frame under the motor. Sometimes these were held in place by spring-loaded clips, but on this car they were bolted on. We saw at once that the bolts were clean and had been off recently. Also, when we got to it, we found that the cast aluminum oil pan was nice and clean. So we took the cap off number three rod and found a turn of leather in it, to replace the Babbitt insert that had burned out! Frank had heard the rod start to rattle and had made the temporary repair at his summer cottage in the country. There was no harm done to the crankshaft.

Going back to Jerry Jackson, he drove a very old Model T. I think that through the years he had purchased almost every accessory and gas-saving device he ever saw advertised. And what is more, he claimed they all did what they were supposed to! He should have been using no fuel whatever.

One thing I remember was a set of coils made integral with the four spark plugs. These were not used for long. Another thing he tried was a dozen or more different types of commutators, each with its patent rotor. This gadget was a fairly touchy business on the Model T. Really, I think the original equipment was probably as good as any of the "improvements," which all sold for two to five times as much.

Another thing Jerry's car was equipped with was a fine pair of acetylene driving lights. These cars had magneto lights, and the higher the engine revolutions the brighter the lights. On bad roads where you were forced to go slow, low gear was often used to get good lights.

While at Bruce Stewart's we did a lot of swimming, as we were right on Charlottetown Harbour. We often ate our lunch while working, then were ready to get into our swim gear as soon as possible after the noon whistle blew. We always had a good diving board and quite a few of the fellows from the machine shop, forge, or foundry swam with us. At the ten to one whistle we all left the water, dressed, and were ready for work at one o'clock.

In colder weather we played poker, penny-ante. And we made as much fuss about losing or winning ten or twenty cents as I saw made by men in western Canada over ten or a hundred dollars when I was there some years later. And I bet we had more fun.

While at Bruce Stewart's, and with the water just outside the garage door, Percy and I, together with a fine young fellow, "Hap" Moore, became very much interested in boating. So we three decided to build a boat. Hap would build the boat. Percy and I would supply the engine and other expensive brass or bronze parts. Work progressed pretty well on schedule until one day in March, Hap informed us that he was broke, but required more lumber for the boat. Four dollars would be enough. We were standing outside the garage watching the ice breaking up. Probably it was later than March. Someone mentioned that we would soon be swimming. Hap said that if each of us gave him two dollars he would jump in!

Percy and I agreed, but had to go to the office to borrow the two dollars each. Art Small held the money. Hap asked for the loan of my bicycle, and could he remove his long rubber boots. He positioned the bike by the side of the garage, watched for an ice floe to move away, and over he went. Needless to say he didn't linger long in the water, on the ladder up, or on the wharf when he had reached it. He grabbed the money from Art, jumped on the bicycle and took off for his home.

Very shortly we saw him leaving Duchemin's lumber mill dressed in his Sunday best and with a few boards over his shoulder. The boat was finished in time for Percy and me to have the engine and hardware installed before the boating season.

Actually I do not recall much about this boat. We used it for one summer, during which Percy and I bought for five dollars an old racing hull formerly owned by Bruce Stewart and Co., and raced to help promote sales for their marine engines. It had been hauled up on a nearby wharf and nearly forgotten. The sun and weather had opened up its planking so that the grass grew under it almost as well as around it.

We should probably have done some painting on it or in it where it was but were advised not to. So we got help to roll it over the wharf and into the water and towed it around to the back of the garage, where we let it soak for some time. Then on Hap's advice we hoisted it out and painted it with Ever-jet, a product that Hap had great faith in.

Then we went ahead and fitted it with a newly overhauled Model T engine and the necessary hardware, and eventually launched it. With Percy at the engine and myself at the rudder and Hap and a few spectators on the wharf, we left the area in a fine burst of speed.

Hap claimed she sailed right out of the paint. In any case, she leaked at almost every seam and we had a lot of work to do on the hull before we could leave it in the water overnight. However, we eventually did get it fairly tight. And she sure was fast, for those days at least.

One Sunday, four of us sailed out of the harbor and straight for Governor's Island, where some company was boring a well in a search for oil. We knew nothing of the depth of the water and a few hundred yards from the island we hit on a shallow rocky ledge, bending the propeller badly. I rolled up my trouser legs and got out and pushed the boat off the rocks. Then we started straight for the Governor's Island wharf again. We should have backed away and gone around a few acres of eel grass, which wound up in the damaged prop and slowed us down to a crawl.

We eventually made it to the wharf, where some kind workmen hoisted the stern out of the water and removed the propeller. Some very skillful man went to work on the damaged wheel and made such a fine job of straightening it that when I later took it to a machine shop they couldn't improve on it.

The men then pointed out the proper direction to take back to Charlottetown, where we arrived without further trouble.

One of the passengers on that trip was Belle MacNeill, who later became my wife!

Dr. Genge, an old sea captain, was on the wharf when we pulled in. He was horrified when he heard where we had been. "You should thank the Lord to be back safely, and don't go again!" he said.

This boat also only lasted one season. It was never really tight.

AN OLD "MO-PED"

That summer, I bought an old bicycle with the main parts of an old motor on it. If I recall correctly it was a Smith Motor Wheel. I paid fifteen hard-earned dollars for it. There was no ignition system on it so I went to the Model T for inspiration. With a Model T timer on the side of the motor, a "buzz" coil and a set of dry cells, I soon had the engine running.

This motor drove the rear wheel of the bicycle by a V-belt to a pulley bolted to the rim. The pulley was nearly as large as the rim. The clutch was an idler wheel on an arm that tightened the belt. The crank arms had to be given a slight offset to provide clearance for the engine. A two-compartment tank suspended from the crossbar contained oil and gasoline. Lubrication was by controlled drip from this tank to the base of the motor. The battery and coil box were strapped to the parcel carrier. This rig always worked well but lacked speed and power.

EARLY SNOWMOBILE

So well did this motorized bicycle work that when winter came, I decided to put it on an ice sleigh. I had some old bicycle parts and I made a three-runner sleigh, patterned largely from the sailing iceboats then in use. The single runner was at the rear and the driver's seat was just over it. The old bicycle frame was pivoted between two two-by-threes that connected the forward cross member to the rear seat. In place of a tire on the bicycle wheel I used a band of steel with spikes to engage the ice. This rig was good on ice but lacked power for use on snow.

HARVEST EXCURSION

Back around this time, the CNR ran cheap trips to western Canada each summer. The fare was ten dollars to Winnipeg and you paid a bit extra to go further. So the accommodations were what you might expect. The passengers were pretty rough, so why give them good seats to tear up? Not knowing much of this, I decided on impulse to go. An acquaintance in Charlottetown was to go as well but didn't show up at the station. However, at Emerald Junction I met a couple of cousins and several schoolmates from up Greenmount way. One of them, George Rayner, stayed with me during the entire trip, which we consider one of the great experiences of our lives.

The first notable adventure was at Montreal, where there was a stopover long enough for us to see a bit of the city. We came across a showroom where the Brooks steam car was on display. They had one on the street, and George and I accepted a drive around the block. This was a very beautiful sedan with the entire body covered with leatherette, with trim of polished aluminum. It was quite a thrill to be speeding along the street with no more than a *swish* of sound. Some say now that the promotion and sale of stock in this company was uppermost in the minds of its chief executives and that they made a lot of money before going bankrupt.

John Getson, a schoolmate of mine, got involved with some other promotion in Montreal and missed the train. When we arrived at Winnipeg much later, John met us at the station very dirty and tousled. He had "rode the rods" of a faster train.

Somewhere in Ontario, probably north of Lake Superior, our train was on a siding waiting for a through train. The conductor told us we would be there half an hour or more and he would have the whistle blown in lots of time. He said the hills were full of blueberries, so dozens of us scrambled up the slope to gorge on them. I never before or since saw blueberries like those, just like small grapes and very thick.

We had a stopover of an hour and a half in Winnipeg. I patronized a barbershop and got a shave. Most of the boys went to a shooting gallery that was a front for some sort of girlie show.

A number of the men had been out on a previous excursion and were getting off at Gull Lake, where they had a good chance of getting work with previous employers. So George and I stopped there also. The station platform was lined with farmers who picked up a crew and took them to their homes. An obliging fellow who had his old crew took us south about eighteen miles and put us up for the night. He also gave us breakfast. He pointed to a house across the prairie where he said we might find work. We insulted him by offering him pay for drive, bed and breakfast.

When we talked with Oscar Von, to whose house we had been directed, he explained that it would be a week or two before his harvest would be ready and that in any case he had promised some Americans who had worked for him the previous year that he would hire them again. He said, however, that his brother, Will, who lived some miles away, might be able to use us, as he had a field of oats that was nearly ripe. He asked us if we could drive a car. We assured him that we could. He pointed to the garage and told us to take his car and go talk to Will. If he had work for us we could bring the car back and his brother could come and get us. If he didn't want us, he might have some other idea.

When we opened the garage door we found a new and very impressive-looking Chevrolet. We could hardly credit that people could be so nice and kind.

Will wasn't at home. His wife told us that he was down in a coulee repairing a windmill. So off we went again in the new Chevy. When we reached the windmill Will said, "I know that's Oscar's car so he must have sent you here looking for work." He asked us a few questions and told us to return the car and he would pick us up after dinner. We had a real fine dinner at Oscar's.

These people had emigrated from Germany just prior to World War One and they sure knew how to cook and eat. Again, they wouldn't accept remuneration.

Will soon arrived and took us to his home. The first job he had us do was to convert a small granary into a bunkhouse. Before evening, their daughter brought us blankets, quilts, and pillows. With lots of straw on the floor inside a board to hold it in place, our beds were complete.

They had a large field of oats, not quite ripe, so we did odd jobs for a couple of days. The first, in answer to one of the questions Will had asked us when he first talked to us, was to go down a deep well to repair the plank walls that were breaking here and there due to outside pressure. There were a number of planks across from side to side where it had been repaired before. George wouldn't go down so I put on a safety rope and went down from cross plank to cross plank. When I found a plank that showed signs of bulging inward, I would have George lower a piece of plank to spike over it, and another one cut to a few inches longer than the diameter of the well. I would drive the latter into place at an angle from wall to wall and spike it, then continue down to the next weak spot. I forget the depth of the well but it was deep. A scary job, but I had assured Will that I would do it. I'm thinking it was about a thirty-foot depth.

He had also asked me if I knew anything about pouring Babbitt, and just coming from a garage, I told him I did. At Bruce Stewart's I had frequently helped Percy Acorn pour new bearings in different things, drive shafts in the machine shop and occasionally a stationary engine. But now the job was on the drum shaft of the threshing mill! I sure was less than happy about the job. Mr. Voll had a plumber's torch and I used the old Babbitt from the boxes, supplemented by bits and pieces picked up from a box of junk. It all went perfectly though, and a very thin shim taken out after the crop was threshed left it in perfect shape for the next year.

We also helped to make some repairs on a windmill on quite a high tower but I don't remember all the details.

The crop of oats was ripe by then. George and I and Mr. Voll were the crew, the last-named on the horse-drawn binder, George and I stooking, which was done with pitchforks. The womenfolk brought drinks to us in the field twice daily. They would ask us at breakfast what we preferred. Meals were eaten with the family except for a cup of coffee and a biscuit early in the morning and milk and cookies and cake at night, which was brought to our bunkhouse.

One amazing thing in our minds was our "bags" of drinking water taken to the field with us. They told us to set them out of the wind but in the sun. Even on the hottest day the water was always cold.

When we threshed, each of us had a team and a wagon and built the load from the ground as we pitched it on—a big change from the way Dad and I had done it. Dad built the loads on his knees and I pitched it on sheaf by sheaf. I always had to keep track of where he was on the load and try to throw the sheaves so the butts were out. This was quite difficult when the load got high and I couldn't see him from close to the wagon.

But the racks on these western wagons were easy to build on and we soon got able to build quite a good load.

We eventually finished threshing the Voll's harvest and worked south. We generally had a job before we left the other so seldom missed a day. One job was with a steam-driven rig owned by a man who did custom work. This outfit had a bunkhouse, a cookhouse, and another trailer for fuel, and the whole outfit made up quite a train as it was hauled across the prairie by the huge steam tractor. When it moved from one farm to another we on the wagons could go on ahead, have a load ready and a few hours' sleep before they were there and had the rig set up.

The last job was jinxed due to snow. We were five weeks idle and without pay but were well fed and housed. Finally the farmer let us go. We drove by horse and sleigh twenty miles to Shaunavon in very cold weather—twelve of us, with only summer underwear on. We mostly ran alongside the sleigh, only taking turns to drive the team that was hitched tandem.

At Shaunavon we found it hard to get lodging. Our train didn't leave till the afternoon of the next day. We finally got a room where three of us had to share a room with a stranger. There were two beds, one already taken. I was the only one of our three willing to bed down with whoever it was that was to occupy the second bed.

We were all tired and went to bed early. When the fourth lad came we all introduced ourselves. He told us the landlady had told him when he took the bed that he might have to share it so he was not surprised. He was a fine boy who knelt by the bed to say his nightly prayer and got in bed and promptly went to sleep, as did I after so long a trip.

To go back to our five weeks of idleness; I mostly read or wrote letters, took long walks, curried and brushed the team of horses that had been assigned to me, cleaned and polished harness, etc. George played poker, which he had played for the first time on the train going out. I had resolved that I wouldn't play out west, as I didn't believe in gambling—penny-ante notwithstanding.

With George, however, it was a horse of another color. He had learned well and had played quite a bit with other outfits. His luck had been fair until he met up with this crew, then it turned awful. He lost consistently, borrowed all I would lend him and lost that, then sold his watch and lost the money.

Now you must remember that we had been on the harvest fields for some time. We had made all we were to make before returning to Prince Edward Island, so his loss was considerable. He was so good-humored about it though that when his luck turned and he won all the loose money in the bunkhouse, no one ever got sore at him. He bought back his watch, repaid me, bought a suit from a fellow, then relieved him of the money! Bought a watch from another guy then cleaned him of the price of it. When we left for home, compared to me, George was a wealthy boy.

We had been privileged to view some really big-time games while with previous outfits. One Saturday afternoon we had driven a couple of loads of wheat to the elevator for a farmer. When the boss had sold the wheat, he stabled all three teams and arranged with us to meet him at midnight. George and I went to a dance. Through the evening we found out that there was a poker game in progress upstairs. We went up and watched for a while. Our fanner was among those playing and as far as we could see, he wasn't doing very well. Some of the pots contained thousands of dollars. We returned to the dance.

At one time George and I exchanged our return tickets with two chaps from British Columbia who had a yen to visit the east, while we thought a trip to the west would be fun. Before we moved on, these boys got a bit homesick I think. It may have been mutual, as I don't recall any trouble in making the second swap.

A number of the boys who went out on those excursions never returned except for a visit in later years. One of these was John Getson, previously mentioned as having missed the train at Montreal. He homesteaded property in Alberta.

THE "BUG"

Back home, I once more went to work with Bruce Stewart & Co., this time spray painting cars. This process by Duco was just coming into vogue. I was sent to a paint shop in St. John, NB. With a bit of foresight I would have stayed away from this very hard work. At that time, as I soon found out, a painter spent but a few minutes a day actually spraying. The rest of the day he was stripping, scraping, sanding, or, with Duco, polishing. Bruce Stewart's spent a lot of money equipping a paint shop, and I always felt it was up to me to make it pay, even if I killed myself at it. We had to compete with some highly skilled old-school carriage painters who could turn out a beautiful car with paint and varnish applied with a brush and striped by hand. On the other hand, a car being repainted with Duco had to be cleaned off to the bare metal, the metal treated against rust with a chemical, the chemical then washed off with hot water or steam, dried with compressed air that was carefully filtered, then immediately given a coat of primer, which was usually red in color. Then followed three or more coats of filler, more where there were roughly soldered seams. This was wet-sanded until glossy smooth. Any places where the prime coat started to show before they were perfect had to have additional coats of filler, then more sanding.

When the whole unit was smooth, three coats of the selected color were applied. Then more sanding, the wet sandpaper being dipped in clear gasoline. When all blemishes were gone, two more coats of paint were applied. Then polishing, first with a fairly coarse polish, then a very fine type until it shone like a mirror. The tips of my fingers were constantly worn to the quick.

Most cars then had artillery wheels (wooden spokes), and open cars with cloth tops had varnished bows or metal ones painted the color of the car. These had to be refinished to match the new color or given a coat of clear Duco. Occasionally the instrument cluster on the dash had to be stripped and refinished to match the car.

Good helpers were hard to get. Most would soon tire of the everlasting sanding and polishing, and most of all the tedious job of removing the original paint.

While at this work I was using my bicycle with the little engine on it. A fellow who had an old Model T Ford traded it for the motor of my bike. I gave him fifteen dollars to boot, and was a very proud boy as I drove my car home.

Someone had removed the back half of the body and had sort of a platform in its place. I used it as it was through the summer and it worked very well.

However, I had other ideas for this car. I had subscribed to a magazine, the *Ford Owner Dealer* and I gleaned a lot of knowledge from them above what I had learned in trade schools. I decided to build a body and to convert the motor and chassis to a more sporty type.

The previous winter I had removed the motor from Father's Model T and had taken it into the large back porch at our house on Admiral Street. Through the long winter evenings I had "lapped" an oversized set of pistons into it, ground the valves and snugged up all the bearings. This motor proved to be very powerful and satisfactory. Cars were not usually used during the winters back then but were "blocked up" and the battery put in a warm place. Then the horse and sleighs were put into very acceptable use.

So now I did the same with my motor except that I had learned a few things from reading. Pistons and rods were carefully balanced for weight by removing metal from the heavier ones. An auxiliary oiling system was used and counterweights were bolted to the crankshaft. A Bosch DU-4 high-tension magneto was used for ignition. This was mounted on a new timing gear cover made for the purpose. This was considered the very tops in ignition systems and did away with the four vibrator-type coils and low tension magneto. However, the latter was still used for lights.

But the big money was spent for an overhead valve head and a new carburetor. The rocker arm cover was of polished aluminum and with the two-inch Stromberg carburetor mounted alongside it up high it sure made an impressive-looking motor. And the power was just as impressive! The valves were very large and the muffler was part of the package so didn't cut down on power much. It was of cast iron and would last indefinitely. The intake manifold was heated by bypassing some of the exhaust around it.

In the spring, this beautiful engine was put in an underslung chassis. The underslinging idea came from an article in *Ford Owner Dealer* and I had some help from a very fine blacksmith, Simon Paquet, and it proved its worth many times over as it made the car very stable and steady. Also, I could change the driveshaft pinion in just around thirty minutes. With regard to this pinion, Ford put out two of them, one with thirteen teeth and one with twelve, which they called the sedan gear. They were interchangeable without further adjustments. By experience I found the car faster and more fun with the "slower" pinion, which I continued to use. I also used a large Gabriel snubber in the center at the rear and a smaller one up front. The roads were mostly clay and gravel then and I have not driven any car that was more stable or rode and steered better. And, for the times, it was extremely fast.

The body was next and was built by myself in an unused part of Bruce Stewart's garage. A wooden frame well braced at all joints was covered with galvanized iron. A door was provided on the passenger side only. The windshield frame was of wood, grooved to take the glass and pivoted near the center for ventilation. The top and side curtains were eventually made by Rodd, a specialist in that work. The paint job was red Duco, changed to cream when the top was made.

Of course, this car never had a battery. Lights were from the regular Model T magneto and were quite adequate when going fast. For several years this car was the fastest one on PEI.

In the winter of 1922, a Durant dealer in Sydney was challenged by our local Hudson agent. The Sydney man claimed their new Essex was faster than the Hudson Terraplane. So they agreed to a race on the ice of Charlottetown Harbour. They staged the race for a Saturday afternoon. Bob MacNeill and I went to watch and to show off, as I could readily outrun them both. However, I had the misfortune to shear a key in the pinion and drive shaft. We debated about what to do, and decided to replace the key. Bob towed me to the garage, where I pulled the rear end while he went looking for a key. We were back on the ice within an hour.

The Hudson dealer was also the editor of the *Evening Patriot*. The next day an editorial in that paper was about the certain car that was so fast on the smooth and level ice surface due to its high-speed gearing. He said that this car wouldn't do so well on the hilly PEI roads. This was about me with the sedan pinion. This man drove a fine Packard coupe which he had always kept in beautiful condition.

I watched for Mr. Gaudet all through the following summer and I finally overtook him on a very hilly clay road. I passed him on a hill, let him pass me on the level or downgrade, then easily passed him on the next hill. The unpaved road was dry and dusty, and I took and gave him plenty of our famous red dust. But he knew what it was all about.

Belle's brother Bob loved to drive this car. One day he and a friend were driving while Belle and I sat in the back. I had prepared myself with a suitable ring, which I was reasonably sure she wouldn't refuse. So while driving along the country road I presented her with this token of our mutual willingness to share our lives, cars, etc., for as long as we lived. She accepted, and we have never regretted it. At least I haven't.

We had many fine trips in this car, the best of all being our honeymoon. Not that we ever went very far as distance goes today. But we got more enjoyment out of this auto than from any we have had since.

WHITE "MICE" AND OTHER PETS

I bought a pair of sweet little white mice one day while working at Bruce Stewart & Co. Took them home and watched them grow into rats! However, they were clean and tame and a lot of fun to have.

I overdid it a bit perhaps one Sunday morning when I took them to church. Harold Harper and I were enjoying their company in a rear seat when we were tapped on the shoulders by Humphrey Arthur, a fine old gentleman who thus indicated that we were to take up the offering that morning. I couldn't put them in a pocket as they would quickly poke their heads out with their whiskers twitching and their pink eyes twinkling as they looked for mischief. So I put both of them up the right sleeve of my jacket. To keep them from coming out around the lapel I had to hold my arm tight to my body, and to keep them from backing down my sleeve I had to hold my left hand at my right elbow. Their tails were long. Harold kept trying to get my eye from the opposite aisle. I was somewhat relieved to be through the job and back in my seat at the rear.

This pair eventually produced a family and, as with the pet fox of two years earlier, the daddy rat got cross. So the cat got the whole business.

Speaking of cats brings memories of what must have been one of the finest cats ever, our own "Lums." We started to call her Kitty Lums but soon shortened it to one syllable. She was definitely my cat, and always slept at the foot of my bed—on top of the covers in the summer, and under them in the winter. She was a fine mouser and knew how to handle a rat so that no matter how many broke cover and ran, not one would escape. A split-second was all it took her to kill one and jump after the other.

I don't think she ever had a batch of kittens anywhere but in the house. We all tried to keep her in the barn as the fateful day approached. But eventually she would be found proudly feeding a new family in Mother's hatbox, a quilt box, or on a bed. Only Mother would be cross. But as the kittens were always cute, she couldn't stay cross long.

Lums would sleep on the oven door occasionally, and once at least she slept in the oven! Father started a fire in the range and shut the oven door before going to the barn to "feed up." Someone heard a racket and rushed downstairs and opened the oven door. A badly scorched cat jumped out. Lums never went near the oven again.

I mentioned earlier that this cat raised seven fox pups in one spring for Perley Haywood.

This cat lived with us for a number of years after we moved to Charlottetown. One bright summer day as I returned to work at noon she was lying in the sun on the front verandah. I stopped a bit to stroke her. She was purring very loudly but didn't get up. I thought nothing of it. However, when I returned that evening she was still there, but had died through the afternoon. I have no idea why she died but I guess she died of old age, and quite contented and happy.

A collie dog, Hunter, also was brought with us to Charlottetown. He and Bob the pet fox had been pups together. Hunter was a great help to us when a fox escaped from any pen into the outside ranch. He would quickly run them down, then stand over them until Dad or I took charge. He was very gentle with them. But the lifespan of a dog is short. They are never with us long enough.

THE RAYNERS

I have previously mentioned a number of Rayners, so I believe they as a whole should have a chapter devoted to them.

Mother's maiden name was Irene Maude Rayner. She had two sisters and five brothers. They nearly all had quite large families, so I had a goodly number of cousins. Some of them lived next door (Aunt Nan's house) and went to school and to the church in Greenmount with us. And Uncle Al was one of Father's partners in fox farming. Their only son, Ernest, was some years my senior. The eldest daughter, Dorothy, died in a diphtheria epidemic.

Ernest was in college, but during summer vacation he had a lovely sailboat and we—or I—enjoyed sailing with him. One time while Ernest was home, Dad brought a barrel of flour to them from Tignish. It was at the rear of the truck wagon. As soon as he stopped the horses, Ernest lifted the barrel off and set it on the ground. Dad made some remark about it being easy that way. Quick as a wink Ernest picked it up and put it back in the wagon. "Now, Uncle Herbert," he said, "it's up to you to take it off this time."

The two girls, Grace and Irene, were company for my two sisters. They did a lot of things together—swam, picked berries in season, and generally had a good time. We all went to school together at Kildare Cape.

Mother's other sister, my aunt Emily, always lived in Worcester, Massachusetts, but visited us at "The Capes" frequently. She had a daughter and two sons.

Three of Mother's brothers lived in Greenmount and Alberton and attended the church at Greenmount. It was my special pleasure to have some of their family come home from morning service or for me to visit with them. It was a special pleasure to go to Uncle B. I.'s (Benjamin Isaac's), as their lively home and barns were very modern and they had a lot of interesting things to see. Domestic water for house and barn was pumped to tanks in the various places by a hydraulic "ram." Their electricity was from a plant of their own. They had their own sawmill and were agents for a lovely type of farm tractor, the Cleveland, later the Cletrac. They had a pleasure motorboat kept in a boathouse that straddled the stream.

Uncle B. I. had an office in Summerside, and the boys, with the help of a hired man, ran the farm and took care of the fox ranch. The children were Ethel, Silas, Ralph, Emily, Lena, Bill, and B. I. Junior. The boys were very mechanically inclined and athletic. As I mentioned earlier, Ralph, who was nearest my age, went to the Agricultural College in Charlottetown the same winter as I.

Uncle Jim, who lived in Greenmount, had a large family as well. Amanda, Ruth, Hennie, Marshall, Helen, Edith, James, and Wallace were the children. They also lost two children in the diphtheria epidemic that took the life of Dorothy Wells. Aunt Freddie and Uncle B. I.'s wife, Sarah, were sisters, and I thought a lot of both of them. They were very kind and were always glad to have me visit at their home.

James, better known to me as Russell, was a wonderful mimic, both of people and animals. He could call birds very expertly. He could go into a person's home and if the woman was upstairs or in another room he could mimic her husband and carry on a prolonged conversation. A real fun place to visit, as they say today.

Then there was Uncle Archie and Aunt Belle, who lived across the road from Uncle Jim, also with lots of children: Hazel, George, Beatrice, Olive, Charlie, Mildred, and Emily. Mildred was drowned at a picnic at the area we called Sou-West, while swimming. A number of others saw her but didn't realize she was in trouble until it was too late.

I visited here most often and in later years, George and I went west on the harvest excursion and were together all autumn.

Uncle Joe and Aunt Lizzie had some trouble and separated. The family was broken up, with the children going to different homes. Weston was taken by his paternal grandparents, Herbert by Aunt Nan, who then lived in Summerside, and others went with people who were strangers to me and I didn't get to know them until years later. Remember, these were horse and buggy days, so it was hard to cover longer distances.

But years later, when Belle and I were en route to Jamaica by boat one time and stopped at Nassau to unload freight, we were hailed by Perley Rayner as we roamed around the straw market. And they

(Perley and his wife) were just in that city for a few hours, by air from Florida. Some coincidence! More about this trip later.

The youngest of my uncles was Uncle E. H. He and Aunt Edith lived in New Annan. Uncle E. H. was a very humorous man with a joke or a story for every occasion. Calhoun, their oldest son, was handicapped in speech and locomotion but was as funny as his father. He lived with us one winter when we had a teacher in our home. And I stayed a week with them in New Annan sometime through the next summer.

This was also quite a large family, at least by today's standards. There was Betty, Virginia, E. H. Jr., Harvey, and I believe there was at least one other. At the time of writing this (1983) I really don't remember as much as I should.

At least two of Mother's sisters died in infancy. And that's about it for my maternal relatives.

HOMEMAKING

Shortly after Belle and I were married, we moved into a house of our own on Esher Street in Charlottetown, where we lived for many years and where we raised our family.

We experienced many joys and a number of heartaches. Death claimed our eldest and our youngest children while we lived there. Sickness added to the busy work of keeping house on a limited budget, and it is a wonder that we are both so well and able to eventually enjoy retirement.

Belle, especially, on whose shoulders fell most of the extra care and labor, and did most of the saving and scraping to make ends meet, deserves everything of pleasure and happiness that we now enjoy.

Two of those years were spent in Montague, where we all made many friends. The children especially were sorry to leave that town when I was transferred back to Charlottetown.

The Dr. Johnston family, made up of a boy to match the age of each of ours, is especially well remembered. Annie and Louie were very good to us during our stay in that lovely town. My work there as a one-man agent for Imperial Oil was difficult. This was during the World War Two period, when gasoline was rationed. The collecting and banking of coupons greatly added to the bookwork. There was no electricity or power of any kind at the plant. All the pumping was done by me on a six-by-six Sarnia pump. The various products would run by gravity into the truck tanks only when the storage tanks were full or above the halfway point. And the products would run by gravity from the railway tank cars into the storage tanks only when the latter were empty to start with. I soon learned to order products early, even though it meant pumping all or nearly all of it. Then it was easier to load into the truck tanks, as all I had to do was sit and watch them fill to the proper level.

Wallace was only age two to four while we were in Montague, so he was too young to be of any help except as enjoyable company for me. But after school or on Saturdays, the older boys could watch the product coming to the gauge while I pumped. Those were the days before metered deliveries. Deliveries were measured by the tankful or by dishing it out by the five-gallon can, kerosene and stove oil especially.

The storage tanks were measured weekly by dipping with a properly chalked tape. On one such measuring day I left Wallace playing in the yard on his tricycle while I climbed the vertical ladder to the top of the tanks. He was then just two years old. While I was gauging the first tank I heard him speak to me. I looked around and there he was, almost up the ladder! It was a wonder I didn't faint or shout. But I realized that the best thing was to let him come on up. I was soon able to get him by the wrist, which was entirely unnecessary except for my peace of mind, as he climbed like a monkey (he still does) and was soon standing entirely relaxed alongside of me.

At that time, all the tanks were connected by a catwalk. I let him stay up with me while I finished gauging. Then I started down ahead of him with my hands on the rung of the ladder just above his. I didn't scold him, either on top of the tank or on the ground. I just made him promise never to climb them unless I was with him.

Customers in Montague called Wallace "The Weaver," as he had the habit of rocking sideways like a metronome, lifting each foot slightly as his body reached the extreme other direction. No, he didn't need to pee!

Although the work was hard and the hours long, we were very happy in Montague. While we moved from one rented house to another (we lived in three while there) we were very happy and enjoyed being there very much. The beautiful river flowed right by our front door for the last year we were there and after doing the books until late at night, Belle and I would often use the boat to row downriver to the post office and return. We would marvel at the wonderful display of phosphorescence at my oar tips and in our wake on moonlit nights.

This boat, the first one of four I built, contributed a great deal to our enjoyment while we lived in Montague. I had a very old single-cylinder Evinrude motor that moved the boat along quite slowly but was dependable and easy to start, so the boys were able to use it. I had another twin cylinder opposed motor but during the war period, parts required to put it into service were not available. Later on, when I did get parts and fixed up the larger motor, I sold the old 1914 motor. I am sorry I did. It was powerful and dependable and would run for hours on only a small tank of gasoline. And it would now be a museum piece of no little value.

BOATS

The boat mentioned in the preceding pages was built of spruce: clean, straight spruce. The plans were run in *Popular Science* or *Mechanics*, I'm not sure now, and some other wood may have been their first recommendation. But spruce was here and was cheap. I made a list of what I wanted, and went to Paoli's Lumber Yard in Charlottetown. The junior Paoli was a yachtsman, and he helped me select the boards. He had a man in the lumber yard tear down a large pile of boards before he had six that suited him.

These boards were not dressed but were a good inch thick. Paoli's didn't have a mill, so I took the boards to Duchemin's. Each one was split in two and dressed to five-sixteenths of an inch thickness, and they were the planks used to make my boat. Plywood of the marine type was unknown then. There wasn't a knot or a flaw of any type in this lovely lumber.

When I was leaving Paoli's with my boards, I tried to thank him for putting himself and his yard man to so much trouble. He said the only thanks he wanted was to see the boat before I put it in the water. And when I took it there later, I think he was as proud of it as I was.

After the war years I was able to get new cylinder blocks for the Fastwin engine, and the combination was pleasingly fast. But this motor was heavy. I could beat Bruce Yeo in a clean race but just barely. He had a more modern four-cylinder Evinrude. But he always had the excuse that my heavy motor was the more powerful.

So one day I suggested that he take my motor and I would use his, and that I might still beat him. He eagerly agreed. His boat was beautifully finished but was much heavier than mine. He had good reason to be proud of it. With the light four-banger on my boat, I really knew what a terrific boat I had. I could outrun Yeo very easily now and the boat ran soft and planed so easily.

With this taste of how my boat could go, I wished for a light, modern engine. My chance to get one came when Eddie Michael bought himself a ten-horsepower Mercury with a "Quicksilver" lower unit (short and very streamlined). But he had a poor boat: it porpoised badly. In an effort to overcome this, he added ten inches to the bottom with some type of trim tabs. Performance was poor and he had some narrow escapes while racing. So he decided to get a family-type boat and I was able to buy the Mercury. Eddie gave me lots of time to pay for it.

And so my first boat was finally wed to an entirely suitable motor. And like the "Bug," the car I enjoyed more than any I was later to own, this was the boat I got the most pleasure from. I won many races and trailored or took it on the roof of our car to many maritime points. Our boys were at an age when they enjoyed it fully as much as I. I could and did enter it in races well above its power class and was never beaten in a race for twenty-five horsepower and under, and often won in unlimited class free-for-alls. I raced it in Montague, Summerside, Souris, Murray Harbour, Sydney, and Halifax, to mention some of the places.

However, as the years passed, boats were being designed and built of plywood, and at Myra Lake (Sydney) I came up against such a boat and was beaten. The week spent at Myra River was a wonderful one. We had found a very lovely place to camp, close by the river and the course used by the Sydney Boat and Yacht Club. I guess Belle didn't appreciate the noise sometimes as the motors were being tried and tuned at all hours, but Douglas, Wallace, and I sure loved the music.

My class race was to have been run on Saturday afternoon but some time was lost due to rain. Finally the weather cleared and the race started, much behind the scheduled time. I won the first heat, which was the first race I had ever run in that was started by a clock. In the second heat I was a bit late crossing the starting line but I came a close second. The third heat was cancelled due to darkness.

The boat that beat me was from Halifax, and the owner couldn't stay to run a third and deciding heat on Sunday morning. I feel I could have won the deciding race, as we were almost exactly equal on the straightaways and my boat was much better on the turns. But his total elapsed time for the two heats was a fraction faster than mine and I had to settle for a second place for the first time in my boat's class.

The winning boat had just been built in Halifax by the driver's father — a new design, and built of mahogany plywood. It was beautifully finished, like a fine piano. It inspired me to build a new hull.

The *Vixen* really proved to be a lot faster, though not as predictable on the corners. I sold the old boat, which I had never named, to Murray White, together with the old Evinrude Fastwin engine, and Murray got years of pleasure out of it. It only went to pieces in the summer of 1975 while it was sitting in his yard on blocks. Some children were playing in it and put the bottom out of it. A really long life for five-sixteenths-inch spruce.

Probably the most exciting race I ever ran with the *Vixen* was off Rustico Harbour. Early in the day, a steering cable broke. Rather than miss the day's fun, I pulled the cables out of their tubes and steered by holding a cable in each hand, the ends going around my arm, over my shoulder to the steering horns on the motor. Then I had to take a passenger to work the throttle, which had to be held open against spring pressure.

Even with a passenger, I readily won the free-for-all. The water was very choppy and rough. I don't know who was the most crazy, the lad holding the throttle wide open or me.

After the race I took a few passengers out, one at a time. One of these was an old friend of mine, Amos Gallant. He was fairly well "lubricated," and when he opened the throttle he held it that way during the completion of the circuit. The boat sure proved itself. The seas were really rough and we were both soaking wet when we were through, but from wind-driven spray. Hardly a cupful came aboard. From this event we took home a lovely car rug.

As previously mentioned, the *Vixen* was not so predictable on the turns, as it slithered about on rough water. Therefore, a lot of races were won the hard way, by keeping well outside on corners until I was well in the lead. In one race in Charlottetown, another boat and I collided and I had my enthusiasm cooled off very quickly. However, I finished overhauling the wet motor and patching the big hole in time for the next week's events.

The *Vixen* is now in Calgary, resting most of the time in Bill's garage. He had some good summers with it but has now graduated to sail. And the motor never worked as well in the more rare air in the foothills. The bottom of this boat, from about a third of the length behind the bow was perfectly flat, so pounded very hard at speed. I have put my knee through the one-quarter-inch plywood floor that was supported by stringers on six-inch centers. In one race I had neglected to remove a quart can of oil and it hit me up between my shoulders before rolling down my back!

Wallace, being much lighter than I, could get more speed out of this boat and when conditions were right, could get it airborne. Only once, on the Montrose River, did I get this thrill. With a fairly stiff breeze and a slight ripple, I headed into the wind. The ripple noise on the bottom sounded like your knuckles rubbed fast on an old-fashioned washboard. Then the noise disappeared and the Mercury screamed an even higher song! I repeated this run several times but couldn't get above the ripple noise. Only on that run did I appreciate the thrill Wallace frequently experienced.

I was never very fat, but often wished to be thinner and lighter so was careful of my diet, especially coming up to that week at Myra Lake.

But we needed a family boat and for this I chose a design that, although hard to build, was to prove a fine boat for the rivers—very stable for a large number to swim from. We have trucked it to every river of any size on the island and have lived aboard it for many long weekends and slept aboard it all summer at New Dominion during the time we were building our home here.

While sleeping aboard I would have breakfast aboard, swim ashore to dress and go to work, leaving Belle to drift ashore when she wanted to come in. With the autumn the water got too cold for swimming, so I hurriedly build a punt. It proved to be a lovely thing to row and I use it almost daily in the summer and fish quahogs and oysters from it in season.

Next I bought a sailing catamaran. The dealer had sold many of these that were short of parts due to breakage, so he had robbed one kit to supply parts for others. I bought what was left when the manufacturer went out of business. I had a local foundry cast some fittings and made others. I soon learned to appreciate the thrill of silent sailing.

THE "INTERVAL"

One of the most pleasant camping trips we had when our boys were relatively young was one we spent in the Middle River area of Nova Scotia.

We had no tent. Our car was an older Plymouth with what they now call suicide doors: the back doors opened to the rear. I had put together a frame of pipe from the gutter of the car roof to a leg, over which I draped a tarpaulin, with the doors opening into the "tent" so formed.

Coming along toward evening as we were driving, we turned into a side road and then into a farm lane. We asked the man of the house if he knew of a good place to park for the night. He directed us to an "interval" where he had just cut and coiled the hay. He told us we could pile as much hay as we liked into one sleeping place.

We followed his directions and drove down across his farm to the river, which he assured us we could readily ford. Then around a bush we came to a small field enclosed by a loop of the river and some trees—the interval. We had never heard this description of such an area but it sure was a very lovely spot. With a couple of coils of newly cut hay piled into the tent and the children asleep on the car seats, we sure had a fine sleep.

In the morning, the boys and I were chasing some tommycod in the river as we swam in it. We found a deep, clear hole and the boys swam and played in their birthday suits. I got some good pictures.

We often pass very close to that farm but have not stopped, afraid that it may have changed.

CABOT TRAIL

This overnight stay at the interval was on the start of a trip around Cape Breton Island and the Cabot Trail. This drive has continued to be our favorite for weekend excursions. But this first, with an old car, little by way of camping equipment, unpaved roads, and the steep hills of those days, was a real adventure. Probably better enjoyed than later trips made with nights spent in campers or motels. In the earlier trips, as soon as we left PEI Belle would start looking for snakes or bears. She slept with a hatchet under her pillow and I had the feeling that she envied the children with their beds in the car seats.

One night in a beautiful area on the Cabot Trail she awakened me to say that a snake was crawling over her bed. She had a flashlight next to the hatchet and when she flashed it on, sure enough there was a mouse crossing her bed. She was so relieved that she turned off the light and I guess she went to sleep. I know I did.

Bobby was the wanderer of our boys, and as far as we were concerned, he often got lost, though he might not have thought of himself as lost. We spent a lot of anxious hours looking for him. He always turned up, and apparently knew where he was all the time. One time, at a fire look-out site on top of a very high hill, he turned up missing. In looking for him, I went down one side of the hill. I slithered down to the meadow at the base, but no sign of him. I climbed back, often on my hands and knees. I met him coming up the road from the other direction, as unconcerned as if he hadn't caused his parents and his grandfather, who was with us on that trip, to age ten years.

On another occasion, after a lot of searching, we heard him call. This time he had worked his way into a swamp and was standing high and dry on a small hummock, but couldn't get off without getting wet. How he had gotten to where he was I couldn't see. He had his shoes on, and was clean and dry.

(Typist's note: end of the book to date. I will send the original "Nothing Book" back to Father right away and tell him to keep going. W. Platts, Nov. 19, 1988.)

(Update at this time of actually going to formal publication. Father made some half-hearted attempts to write more, but it lacked the pioneering adventure of his earlier stories. We called it quits. It's perfect as it is. Father and Mother lived a good, long life, dying in their 90s in Charlottetown, Prince Edward Island, where they will always be remembered for the fine couple they were. W. Platts, March, 2016.)

Cover Photo: "The Bug", the underslung roadster built by hand by the author: Model T Ford frame and engine, the latter converted to overhead valves and featuring hand-balanced pistons and rods. Special ignition, custom dampers and his hand-crafted aluminum body. Photo by Bob McNeill, brother to Belle — the author's future wife.

Red soil of "the island"

4th of 5 boats built